MINs PERFORMANCE FOR PARALLEL PROCESSING

Prof. Harsh Kumar Sadawarti

aberdeen university
press services

Printed in the United States of America
ISBN: 978-0-6151-7696-3

This book is printed on 6" x 9", perfect binding, 60# cream interior paper, black and white interior ink, 100# white exterior paper, full-color exterior ink. Prices are subject to change.

Cover Title Designed by Aberdeen University Press Services.

MINs Performance for Parallel Processing
First Edition
Harsh Kumar Sadawarti

Dedicated to

My Wife Ritcha

and

Sons Saarthak, Sidhant

ABSTRACT

The Performance of a system depends directly on the time required to perform an operation and number of these operations that can be performed concurrently. High performance computing systems can be designed using parallel processing. The effectiveness of these parallel systems rests primarily on the communication network linking processors and memory modules. Hence, an interconnection network that provides the desired connectivity and performance at minimum cost is required for communication in parallel processing systems. Multistage interconnection networks provide a compromise between shared bus and crossbar networks.

In this thesis, a new class of Irregular, Fault-tolerant multistage interconnection network named as Irregular Augmented Shuffle Network (IASN) has been proposed. The network has less number of stages as compared to existing irregular networks. Various performance parameters have been analyzed which shows better performance of the proposed network than the existing networks. The reliability of a network is evaluated in terms of MTTF. It has been seen the IASN has a higher MTTF for upper and lower bound in comparison to networks such as ASEN-2 and ABN and is compatible to FT network.

The permutation passability determines the data routing capability in the fault-free as well as faulty conditions. This parameter has been analyzed in terms of identity as well as incremental permutations. The results show that IASN is better that ASEN-2 and ABN in terms of average path length. Also IASN is better than the irregular FT network in terms of path length. As well as percentage of requests passed. Moreover, the network is cost-effective too.

Two pass routing scheme is described for communication in a multiprocessor system employing a unique-path multistage interconnection network in the presence of faults in the network. It is capable of tolerating all single faults and many multiple faults in all except the first and last stages of the network. The routing scheme is useful for tolerating both permanent as well as intermittent faults in the network. The hardware over head for implementing the scheme is very small and no time-penalty is paid in the fault-free case.

A new class of irregular fault tolerant multistage interconnection network called the ZT Network has been proposed and analyzed. We will see ZT Network can achieve general goals for the design of a fault tolerant network i.e. good performance even in the presence of faults, high reliability, low cost, all permutation passable, and a simple control scheme.

TABLE OF CONTENTS

CHAPTER 1 : INTRODUCTION

1.1 INTRODUCTION

As designers strive to make more efficient use of scarce bandwidth, the performance of most multiprocessor systems are limited by the interconnection pattern and routing of the communication networks. Despite tremendous achievements in providing fault-tolerance and performance improvisations, demand towards new designs for interconnection networks is gaining prominence to forestall degradation as the network size increases. Concurrent processing of data items is considered as a proper approach for significantly increasing the processing speed of high performance systems.

Today is the era of parallel processing. Parallel processing is an efficient form of information processing which emphasize the exploitation of concurrent events in the computing process. To achieve parallel processing, development of more capable and cost-effective multiprocessor systems are required. Earlier computer designers started with a development of uniprocessor systems. Today we can extend the computer structure to include multiprocessors with shared memory space & peripherals. In such a multiple processing system, processors may spend a considerable amount of time just communicating among themselves unless an efficient interconnection network (IN) connects them

Interconnection networks are currently being used for different applications, ranging from internal buses in very large scale integration (VLSI) circuits to wide area computer networks. Among others, these applications include backplane buses and system area networks, telephone switches, internal networks for asynchronous transfer mode (ATM) switches, processor/memory interconnects for vector supercomputers, interconnection networks for multicomputer and distributed shared memory multiprocessors, clusters of workstations, local area networks, metropolitan area networks, wide area computer networks and networks for industrial applications. The number of applications, requiring interconnection networks, is continuously growing.

Multistage interconnection networks (MINs) are recognised as cost-effective means to provide high-bandwidth communication in multiprocessor systems, as opposed to crossbar switches which are highly efficient but are prohibitively expensive, with O (N2) cost (where N is the number of input/output terminals) and the time shared buses which are inexpensive but have unacceptable throughput when the number of processors connected to them are large.

Multistage interconnection networks (MINs) provide interconnection through a number of switch stages, where each switch is a basic crossbar network. If the number of switching elements (SEs) in each stage are same, the MIN is categorized as regular otherwise it is irregular. A majority of the proposed regular MINs belong to a class of networks which in their basic form, consist of logmN stages of m x m SEs connecting N input terminals to N output terminals. The SEs in adjacent stages are connected by an interconnection pattern that allows any input to be connected to any output. Such MINs have O (NlogN) hardware cost, O (logN) path length, and the ability to provide up to N simultaneous connections. In addition, they can employ simple and distributed routing algorithms which eliminate the need for a central controller and reduce the connection set up time. These properties make MINs attractive for multiprocessor applications.

* Performance evaluation work, on interconnection networks; has been done quite extensively. However, previous evaluation models have been commonly based on the unrealistic assumption that a block request is discarded and independent request is generated to replace the previously blocked and yet unserved request. This assumption helps researchers simplify the theoretical model, but the simplification will result in discrepancies in predicting network performance*

The basic idea, for developing high performance .routing algorithms is to provide multiple paths for input-output pair so that alternate paths can be used in case of faults. It can be achieved by including increasing number of stages, increasing the size of the switches, providing extra stages etc.

The performance of a multiprocessor system is weighed in terms of Bandwidth, Throughput, Probability of acceptance, Reliability, Permutation, Cost, Path length and Fault tolerance.

1.2   STATEMENT OF THE PROBLEM

The general goals, for the design of high performance optimization of Multistage Interconnection Networks (MINs) are high reliability, good performance even in the presence of faults, high computational speed, low cost, less switch delay time and simple control. However, most of the methods, network designs, routing algorithms and connecting techniques proposed in the literature for MINs cannot achieve ail of these goals simultaneously. Most of the regular MINs, proposed in the literature, have path length O (log N), which puts a limitation on the computational speed of a MIN. Some of the networks fail to tolerate faults in the first and/or the last stage. Some others can tolerate faults in any stage, but they cannot maintain permutation capability when any single fault occurs, A few exceptions such as replicated networks and INDRA [Ragh 84] network can maintain permutation capability in case of faults, but they are, in general, too costly.

The main objective of the present research work is to explore the techniques for the design of reliable, computationally faster, fault-tolerant and cost-effective MINs. Routing algorithms for MINs having good performance optimisation has also been one of the objectives. The problem of improving the performance of the existing routing algorithms and networks for MINs has also been considered. Attempts are made to design networks and develop routing algorithm having better performance optimization for regular/irregular MINs compared to that having similar hardware complexity levels for regular/ irregular MINs.

Already much of the work has been done in the field of regular networks but less attention has been paid to irregular networks. Analysis of irregular networks shows that these networks provide good performance in terms of various design parameters, irregular networks are multipath in nature and path length varies depending on the path chosen. Hence, the favorite source-destination pair requests pass through the shortest path length equals to 2, which helps in reducing the latency.

In this thesis, an attempt has been made on irregular networks so as to improve the existing networks and hence to propose a new multistage interconnection network having better performance measures in comparison to the existing networks. And hence, a new class of Irregular Fault Tolerant Multistage Interconnection Network named Irregular Augmented Shuffle Network (IASN) has been proposed in this thesis. The fault tolerance capability of the network helps the network to operate even in presence of some non-critical faults. The network has been evaluated and analyzed in terms of its reliability, performance, permutation passability and cost These parameters have been compared with various existing regular and irregular networks. The results show better performance of the proposed IASN network as compared to various existing networks. Also the irregularity in the network helps 50% requests to pass through minimum path length, which helps in reducing the delay in the network.

Specifically, the problems considered in this thesis can be stated as follows:

- To propose newer and or augmenting the existing networks in order to improve the reliability and performance

- To develop irregular fault-tolerant MINs which are cost effective and have shorter path length compared to regular fault tolerant MINs

- Developing high performance routing algorithms

- Designing high performance networks for minimizing the cost

  of interprocessor communication delay

The efforts, in exploring the above objectives, have resulted in designing of :

- An Efficient Irregular Augmented Shuffle Network
- An Efficient Routing Algorithm.
- An Efficient Irregular ZETA Network

1.3 ORGANIZATION OF THESIS

The general parallel processing concepts, described in Chapter 1-INTRODUCTION.

Brief description of single-stage and multistage networks, performance and reliability

measures of MINs for determining the performance and reliability has been discussed in

Chapter 2 - INTERCONNECTION NETWORKS.The various existing unique-path,

multipath, regular, irregular, static and dynamic MINs have been discussed in Chapter 3 -

SURVEY OF MINs. A detailed survey has been provided in this chapter, which

categorize these networks and helps to know the features available in these networks.

The next chapter, IRREGULAR AUGMENTED SHUFFLE NETWORK (IASN),

describes the new proposed Irregular, Fault tolerant multistage interconnection network.

The reliability, performance and cost analysis of the proposed network has been done

and compared with various existing networks. The permutation passability measures of

the proposed network have been discussed in Chapter 5 - PERMUTATION

PASSABILTY in IASN. Two pass routing scheme is described for communication in a

multiprocessor system employing a unique-path multistage interconnection network in the presence of faults in the network in chapter 6- FAULT TOLERANT ROUTING IN

MINS., In Chapter 7 A new irregular ZETA network has been proposed and chapter 8 -

CONCLUSIONS and FUTURE SCOPE OF WORK gives the concluding remarks of

the thesis, which are followed by highlighting the future scope of multistage

interconnection networks.

CHAPTER 2 : INTERCONNECTION NETWORKS

2.1 INTRODUCTION

Interconnection networks play a central role in determining the overall performance of a system. The interconnection through crossbar is highly efficient but it is expensive as the cost increases with 0 (N^2), N being the network size. Time shared buses are inexpensive but have unacceptable throughput for large number of processors [22].

Hence, in order to provide fast, efficient and reliable communication at reasonable cost in large parallel processing systems, many different networks between the extremes of single bus and crossbar have been proposed. Such interconnection networks can be constructed from single or multiple stages of switches. In a single stage network, data may have to be passed several times before reaching the final destination. In a multistage network, one pass of multiple stages of switches is sufficient

2.1.1 Single-stage interconnection networks

Single stage networks can be viewed as an intraconnected set of N inputs and N output units. Fig 2.1 shows the conceptual model of single-stage network to interconnect an N component parallel processing system.

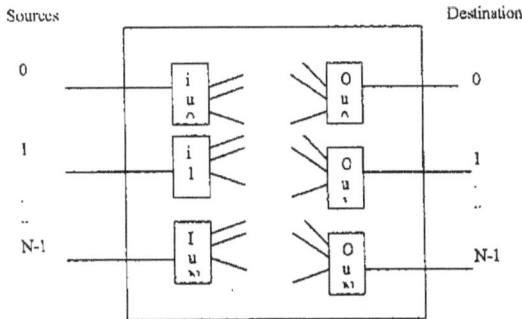

Fig 2.1 Conceptual view of a single stage interconnection network

The way the input units are connected to the output units determines the functional characteristics of the network i.e. allowable interconnections [24].

There are four basic types of single stage networks:

- **Mesh**

- **Cube**

- **Shuffle-Exchange**

- **Plus-Minus 2** [i]

Interconnection networks are defined by the set of interconnection functions. An interconnection function If mathematically maps an address X to address If (X).

- **Mesh Network** : The wraparound mesh network as shown in Fig 2.2 consists of four interconnection functions defined as:

$M_{+1}(X) = X+1$ modulo N

$M_{-1}(X) = X+1$ modulo N

$M_{+n}(X) = X+1$ modulo N

$M_{+n}(X) = X+1$ modulo N

Where N (square root of n) is assumed to be an integer.

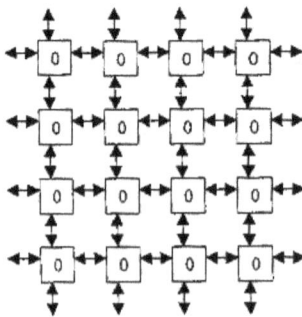

Fig 2.2 Wraparound Mesh network

Fig 2.2 Wraparound Mesh Network

Fig 2.2 Wraparound Mesh Network

- **Cube Network:** The Cube network as shown in Fig 2.3 is defined by $m=\log_2 N$ interconnection functions on the binary representation of the system addresses.

The name cube network is due to the fact that connectivity of this network can be represented by an m-dimensional cube whose corners represent the system component addresses.

In a cube, the vertical lines connect vertices whose way that addresses differ in most significant position. Horizontal lines differ in least significant bit positions.

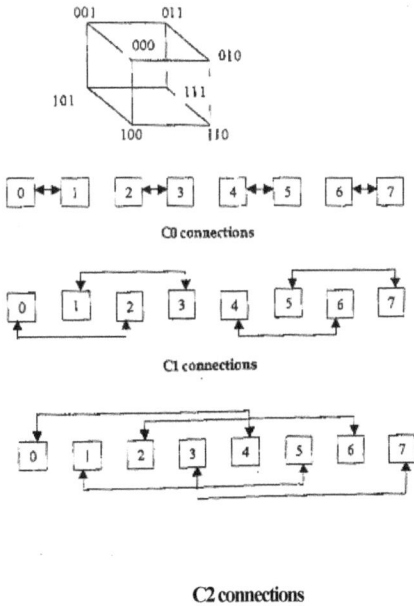

C0 connections

C1 connections

C2 connections

Fig 2.3 Cube Network For N=8

- **Shuffle-exchange network:** Shuffle exchange [25] network is based on routing functions that are Shuffle and Exchange. A perfect shuffle of N=8 is shown in Fig 2.4. Perfect shuffle cuts the deck into two halves from the center and intermixes them evenly. Inverse perfect shuffle does the opposite

to restore the original ordering as shown in Fig 2.5.

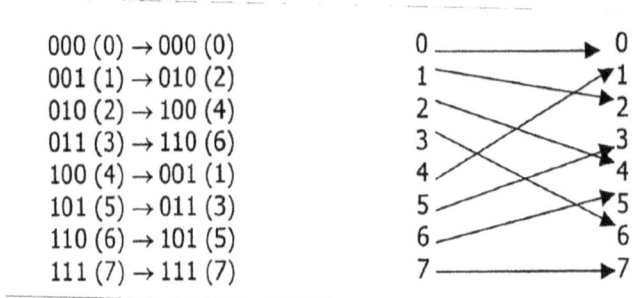

```
000 (0) → 000 (0)          0 ―――――――――→ 0
001 (1) → 010 (2)          1              1
010 (2) → 100 (4)          2              2
011 (3) → 110 (6)          3              3
100 (4) → 001 (1)          4              4
101 (5) → 011 (3)          5              5
110 (6) → 101 (5)          6              6
111 (7) → 111 (7)          7 ―――――――――→ 7
```

Fig 2.4 Perfect shuffle

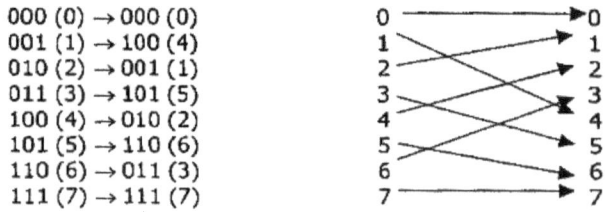

```
000 (0) → 000 (0)          0 ―――――――――→ 0
001 (1) → 100 (4)          1              1
010 (2) → 001 (1)          2              2
011 (3) → 101 (5)          3              3
100 (4) → 010 (2)          4              4
101 (5) → 110 (6)          5              5
110 (6) → 011 (3)          6              6
111 (7) → 111 (7)          7 ―――――――――→ 7
```

Fig 2.5 Inverse shuffle

Plus minus 2^i (PM2I) networks: The interconnection functions of the PM2I network

[24] as shown in Fig 2.6 are:

$PM2_{+i}(X) = X + 2^i$ modulo N

$PM2_{-i}(X) = X - 2^i$ modulo N

PM2+0 connections

PM2+1 connections

PM2+2 connections

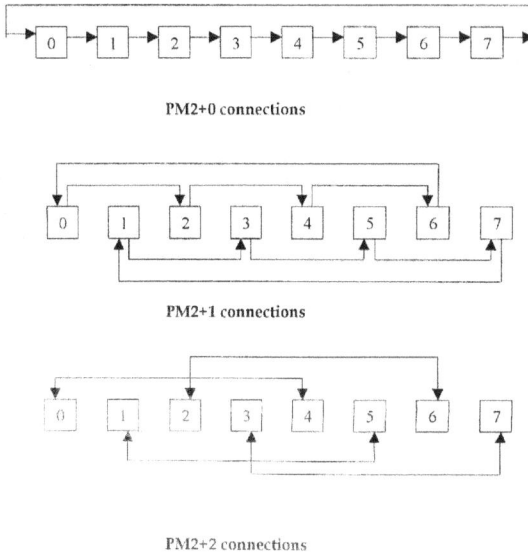

Fig 2.6 PM2I Network for N=8

2.1.2 Multistage interconnection networks

The multistage interconnection networks contain multiple stages of switches linked to one another. These multistage interconnection networks are built from stages of basic single-stage networks. For example, if the basic stages used are cube and shuffle-exchange, then Generalized Cube multistage network is obtained. Networks built from stages of the PM2I interconnection functions are known as Data Manipulator networks. A complete survey of multistage interconnection networks (MINs) has been done in Chapter 3.

2.2 REDUNDANCY GRAPH

Redundancy graph as shown in Fig 2.7 depicts all the possible paths between a source and a destination. It offers a way to study the properties of a multipath MIN, such as the number of faults tolerated or the type of rerouting possible. Nodes on the graph represent the switching elements. If the switching element belongs to the first or last stages become faulty, then the source or destination connected to that particular switching element will be disconnected from the network.

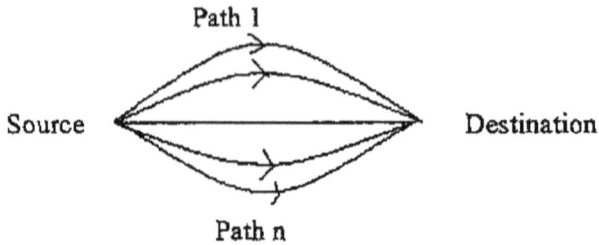

FIG: 2.7 Redundancy Graph

2.3 PERFORMANCE MEASURES OF MINs

The performance measure factors of MINs are:

- **Bandwidth:** It is defined as the mean number of active memory modules in a transfer cycle of interconnection network. It also takes into account the memory access conflicts caused by random nature of processor requests.

- **Probability of acceptance:** It is the ratio of expected bandwidth (i.e. total number of successful requests) to the expected number of requests generated per cycle. In other words, it is the probability that a request generated by a source should be successful in reaching the destination. Thus, it is the ratio of the requests matured to the total requests generated.

- **Throughput:** It is the average number of packets or the maximum amount of information delivered by the network per unit time.

  Processor Utilization: It is the expected percentage of time a processor is active doing internal computation without accessing the global memory.

- **Processing Power:** It is sum of processor utilization over the number of processors and is a simple extension of processor utilization.

2.4 GENERAL MIN MODEL

Assume a MIN of size an x bn constructed from a x b crossbar switches and having an sources connected to bn destinations. The analysis of crossbar is applied to a x b crossbar switch and then extended for the complete MIN. The distinct destination digit (in baseb) for setting of individual a x b switches controls each stage of MIN. Since the destinations are independent and uniformly distributed, so are the destination digits. For example, in some arbitrary stage i, a x b crossbar uses digit dn-i of each request; this digit is not used by any other stage in the network. Moreover, no digit other than dn-i is used by stage i. The probabilistic approach is used to analyze the MINs based on request independent assumptions [10,22]

Given the request rate p at each of the a inputs of an a x b crossbar module, the expected number of requests that it passes per unit time is given by

$$b - b(1 - p/b)a$$

Dividing the above expression by the number of output lines of a x b module gives the rate of requests on any one of the b output lines.

$$1 - (1 - p/b)a$$

Thus, the output rate of request q in any stage of MEN is a function of its input rate and is given by:

$$q = 1 - (1 - p/b)a$$

Since the output rate of a stage is the input rate of the next stage, output rate of any stage can be recursively evaluated starting from stage 1. And the output rate of final stage n determines the bandwidth of MEN. Let qi be the rate of request on an output link of stage i, the bandwidth for an x bn MIN is given by:

$$BW = b^n p_n$$

According to the definition, BW is the total number of requests matured.

$$q_i = 1 - (1 - q_{i-1}/b)^a \ , \ q_0 = q$$

The probability of acceptance of a request is given by:

$P_a = b^n q_n / a^n q$

Throughput (TP): $\qquad\qquad\qquad\qquad\qquad$ $TP = BW / a^n T$

Where T is the average time taken for memory or source read/write operation.

Processor utilization (PU): $\qquad\qquad\qquad\qquad$ $PU = BW / a^n pT$

Processing Power (PP): $\qquad\qquad\qquad\qquad\qquad$ $PP = a^n \times PU$

These performance parameters have been computed for a general MIN model, having any number of inputs or outputs [7,10,22].

2.5 RELIABILITY MEASURES

Reliability of a system is the probability that it will perform its intended function satisfactorily for a given time under stated operating conditions. A well known criteria used to measure the reliability of fault tolerant networks is full-access. Under this criterion, a network is assumed to be faulty if there is any source-destination pair that cannot be connected because of faulty components in the network. Three fault models are used for MINs: the stuck-at fault model, link fault model and switch fault model. In stuck-at fault model, a failure causes a crossbar switch to remain in a particular state regardless of the control inputs given to it, thus affecting its capability to set up suitable connections. In link fault model, a failure affects an individual link of a switch, leaving the remaining part of the switch operational. In the switch fault model, the strongest of the three, a failure of switch makes it totally non-operational Switch fault model is used for the analysis of MINs [4].

Under the criteria of full access, reliability can be measured in terms of Mean Time to Failure (MTTF). The MTTF of a MIN is defined as the expected time elapsed before some source is disconnected from some destination. The analysis is based on the lower and upper bounds of the network reliability [4,7,9,26].

$$MTTF = \int_0^\infty R(t)dt$$

The Probability, $R_{cs}(t)$, of a critical set not being faulty is:

$$R_{cs}(t) = \left[1 - (1 - e^{\lambda' t}) \right]$$

$\lambda' = \lambda$ for 2 x 2 crossbar switch

$k\lambda / 2$ for k x 1 multiplexer or 1 x k demultiplexer

- 14 -

2.6 SERIES AND PARALLEL MODEL FOR RELIABILITY

2.6.1 Series Model

A system consisting of n components is said to be of series type if the functional diagram of the system suggests that the successful operation depends on the proper operation of all the n components. Failure of even a single component makes the system useless [4].

The assumptions for the series model are:

   i. Each component operates or fails independently of every other one, at least until the first component failure occurs.

  ii. The system fails when the first component failure occurs,

 iii. Each of the n (possibly different) components in the system has a known life distribution model Fi (t).

An important characteristic of a series system is that its reliability is always worse than the poorest component in it. Reliability of a series type of system is given by the product of reliabilities of the individual components in it.

$$R_{Series}(t)=R_1(t).R_2(t).R_3(t)...............................R_n(t)$$
$$=\text{PRODUCT [i=1 to n] } R_i(t)$$

$$F_{Series}(t)=\left[1-F_1(t)\right].\left[1-F_2(t)\right]...........................\left[1-F_n(t)\right]$$
$$=1\text{-PRODUCT [i=1 to n] }\left\{1-Fi(t)\right\}$$

Fig 2.8 shows the series reliability model. It shows a system with 5 components in series, which are then replaced by an equivalent system with only one component As shown in the figure, the equivalent system with one component has reliability equal to the product of the reliabilities of individual components.

2.6.2 Parallel Model

A system with n components is said to be of parallel type if and only if the successful functioning of any one of the components leads to the success of the system. The model assumes that all the n components that make up a system operate independently and system works as long as at least one component still works. It is the opposite of series model and in this all the components have to fail before the entire system fails. If there are n components, any (n-l) of them may be considered redundant to the remaining one. The system reaches the failure at the time of last component failure [4].

The assumptions for the series model are:

1. All components operate independently of one another, as far as reliability is concerned

2. The system operates as long as at least one component is still operating, The failure

    of the system occurs at the time of last component failure

3. The component distribution function (CDF) for each of the component is known

In parallel model, the equivalent CDF (Fs (t)) for the system is the product of the CDF's of the individual components.

$F_{parallel}$ (t) = F_1 (t).F_2 (t)......... .... .F_n (t)

$$= 1 - PRODUCT [i = 1 \text{ to } n] Fi (t)$$

$R_{parallel}(t) = [1 - R_1(t)]. [1 - R_2(t)].. ... . [1 - R_n(t)]$

$$= PRODUCT [i = 1 \text{ to } n] \{[1-R_i(t)]\}$$

Fig 2.9 shows the parallel reliability model. It shows a system with 5 components in parallel, which are then replaced by an equivalent system with only one component. As shown in the figure, the equivalent system with one component has reliability equivalent to the product of one minus reliabilities of the individual components.

Series system reduced to equivalent one component system

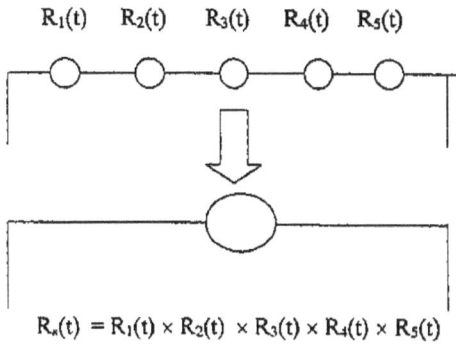

$R_1(t)$ $R_2(t)$ $R_3(t)$ $R_4(t)$ $R_5(t)$

$R_n(t) = R_1(t) \times R_2(t) \times R_3(t) \times R_4(t) \times R_5(t)$

Fig 2.8 Series Reliability Model

Parallel system reduced to equivalent one component system

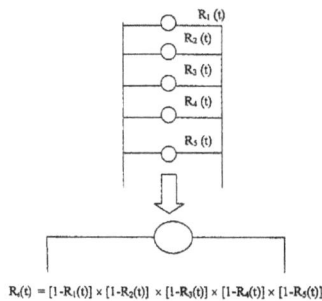

$R_1(t)$
$R_2(t)$
$R_3(t)$
$R_4(t)$
$R_5(t)$

$R_e(t) = [1-R_1(t)] \times [1-R_2(t)] \times [1-R_3(t)] \times [1-R_4(t)] \times [1-R_5(t)]$

Fig 2.9 Parallel Reliability Model

2.7 CONCLUSION

In this chapter a brief introduction about the types of interconnection networks has been discussed in terms of single-stage and multistage networks. Various types of single-stage networks have been discussed which serve as a basis for designing of multistage networks. The complete survey of multistage networks has been done in the next chapter.

Various performance measure factors used to calculate the performance of a multistage interconnection network has been studied which help in determining the performance of multistage interconnection networks. Reliability measures of MINs have been also discussed in this chapter. The series-parallel models used to determine the reliability have been studied for determining the reliability of the MINs.

The next chapter provides a detailed survey of MINs in terms of unique path, multipath, static, dynamic, regular and irregular networks.

CHAPTER 3 : SURVEY OF MINs

3.1 INTRODUCTION

Given the present state of technology, building multiprocessors systems with hundreds of processors is feasible. And the vital component in these systems is interconnection networks that enable the processors to communicate among themselves or with the memory units. Interconnection Network is a complex connection of switches and links permitting processors in a multiprocessor system to communicate among themselves or with memory modules. And the basic function of an interconnection network is to transfer information from input nodes to the output nodes by setting up communication paths.

Interconnection technology is creating an entirely new atmosphere; it is now economically feasible to construct a multiprocessor system by interconnecting large number of processors and memory modules [1,10]. Interconnection networks are currently being used for many different applications such as telephone switches, internal networks for asynchronous transfer mode (ATM) switches, processor/memory interconnects for supercomputers, local area networks, wide area computers, interconnection networks for multicomputers and distributed shared memory multiprocessors and networks for industrial applications. The number of applications requiring interconnection networks is continuously increasing. Therefore, concept, design and implementation of the interconnection networks are the crucial factors to be considered.

The study of interconnection embodies the study of large number of interconnection networks ranging from simple bus to large networks constructed from multiple stages of crossbar switches [11,13]. Multistage interconnection networks (MINs) occur as a compromise between bus based and crossbar networks. The bus-based networks are simple to construct and their cost is low but these networks are not scalable in terms of performance. Similarly, the crossbar networks although scale better in performance than bus-based networks but these networks are very costly. MINs provide more cost-effective communication than crossbar networks and a high bandwidth communication compared to the bus system, Hence, MINs occur as an alternate to the bus-based and crossbar networks. In order to provide fast, reliable and efficient communication at a reasonable cost in large parallel processing systems, many different multistage interconnection networks between the extremes of single bus and the crossbar have been proposed. The study of these multistage interconnection networks involves the detailed study of different types of existing multistage interconnection networks.

The various existing MINs differ from each other in various design parameters. These design parameters include the number of stages, number of switching elements per stage, number of links, auxiliary links used, type of routing, fault tolerance criteria etc. So, these networks have different performance, reliability, efficiency and cost There is no network that can be considered 100% efficient because achieving efficiency in a network involves trade-off between various factors.

MINs can be modeled by a graph G (N, C), N being the number of SEs and C the set of unidirectional or bi-directional links. The pattern of the interconnection may be uniform non-uniform, which classifies the MINs to be regular or irregular. The network may be fault tolerant or non-fault tolerant depending on whether it continues to operate even in presence of faults. Moreover, static MINs have a fixed topology whereas a dynamic MIN allows the pattern of interconnection to very dynamically.

Hence, different networks have been proposed and analyzed by various researchers who have considered different type of networks from different aspects, These networks can be classified depending on whether they are unique path or multipath, regular or irregular. These networks can be also broadly classified into static and dynamic networks [3].

CLASSIFICATION OF MINs

Fig 3,1 Classification of MINs

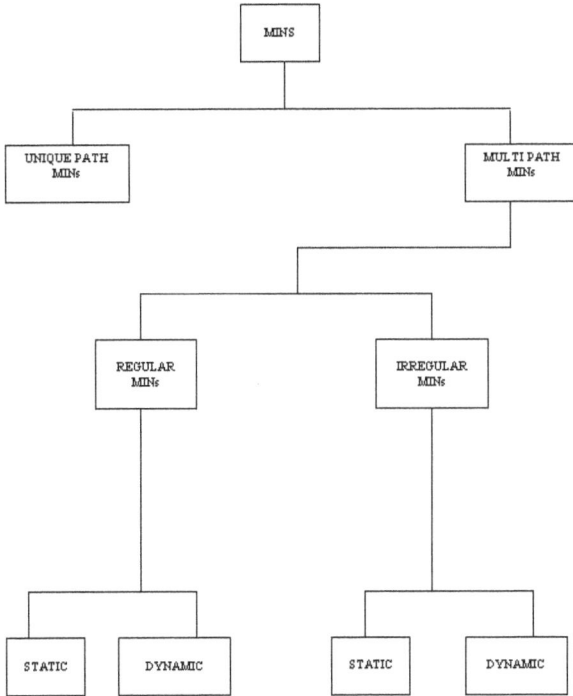

3.2 UNIQUE PATH MINs

Unique path MINs are characterized by the presence of a single path between any source-destination pair. They are not even single fault tolerant and failure of even one of the switches disconnects some of the source-destination pairs.

Some of the properties of unique path MINs are:

1) The hardware cost is of 0 (N log N), providing N simultaneous paths having path-lengths O (log N)

2) They provide simple and distributed routing algorithms making the central routing unnecessary and thus result in low communication latency times

3) A unique path exists between any source to any destination, and distinct source/ destination paths may have common links

Generalized Cube Network [12], Omega Network [16] and Baseline Network [30] are the examples of unique path networks.

3.2.1 Generalized Cube Network

A N x N Generalized Cube network is made up of $m = \log_2 N$ stages, each of which consists of N/2 interchange boxes. The interchange boxes can be in one of the four possible states: straight, swap, lower broadcast and upper broadcast. A two-function interchange box can be in the straight or swap state, and a four-function interchange box can be in any of the four states. Fig 3.2 shows Generalized Cube network for N=8.

The input links to stage m-1 are the network input links but connected to the interchange boxes in such a way that Cm-1 cube interconnection function can be implemented in each interchange box. The output links of the stage m-1 are the input links to the stage m-2, but connected in such a way that the interchange boxes in the stage m-2 can perform Cm-2 cube interconnection function. By repeating this procedure between the stages through stage 0, the connections of the generalized cube are formed.

Main Features of the network are as follows:

For an N x N cube

No. of stages $= \log_2 N$

No. of switches per stage = N/2

Total No. of switches = N/2 $\log_2$N

3.2.2 Omega Network

The Omega network is based on the single-stage shuffle-exchange network. An Omega network of size N consists of m identical stages, each of which consists of a shuffle connection followed by a column of N/2 interchange boxes. Each stage has N/2 switch modules. Each switch module is individually controlled. Various combinations of the switch states implement different permutations, broadcast, or other connections from the inputs to the outputs. The routing is done by inspecting the destination bit starting from the most significant bit (MSB) of the destination address. If the i-th bit of the destination address at stage i is 0, then input is connected to the upper output otherwise it is crossed-over. But the omega network is a blocking network that is when routing requests to different memory banks share a link the message can be blocked by another message. This is because of the unique path property of the omega network. Fig 3.3 shows Omega Network for N= 16.

Main Features of the network are as follows:

For an N x N cube

No. of stages = log2N

No. of switches per stage = N/2

Total No. of switches = N/2 log2N

3.2.3 Baseline Network

The baseline network is also a unique path static multistage interconnection network. The connections are direct Routing of data from source to destination is performed using destination address of the routing tag. For example, the route taken by a source in the unique path Baseline network, having source address sn-1 sn-2,.......... s0 to destination dn-1 dn-2...do will be uniquely specified by the path code as sn-1 sn-2,.......... s0 dn-1 dn-

2…do. Position of the path in any intermediate stage of the Baseline Network can be found by observing an n-bit window in the path code (n=log$_2$N). Fig 3.4 shows the Baseline network for N=16.

Main Features of the network are as follows:

For an NxN Omega Network

No. of Stages = Log$_2$N

No. of Switches Per State = N/2

Total No. of Switches = N/2Log$_2$N

But there are certain problems associated with the unique path MINs. Some of these problems are:

- **No alternate path available:** As there exist only single path between source-destination pairs, so no alternate path is available for routing when failure of a particular switching element occurs in the network. The failures of a single link or switch will cause disconnection of several source/destination paths.

- **Blocking:** Also in the unique path networks, if a particular output link is busy then no other source-destination pair can communicate on the same link. And as no other path is available, it causes blocking of the network when several requests occur simultaneously. So, a source/destination connection that gets blocked by a previously established connection results in poor performance in a random access environment.

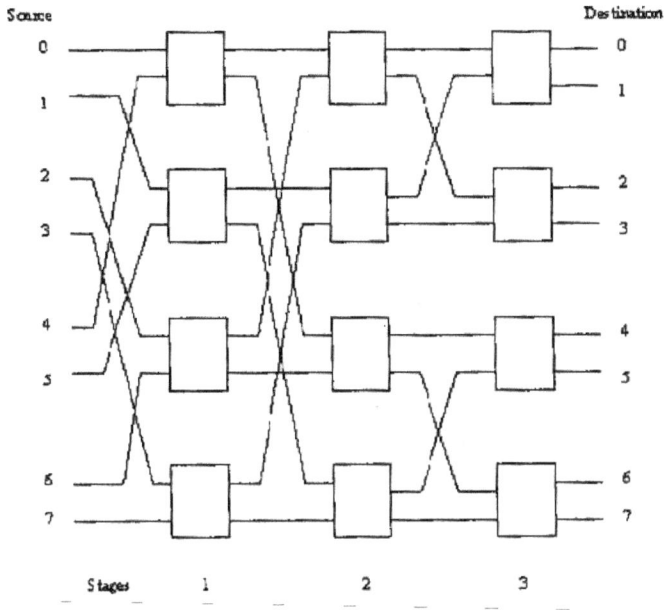

Fig 3.2 Generalized Cube Network

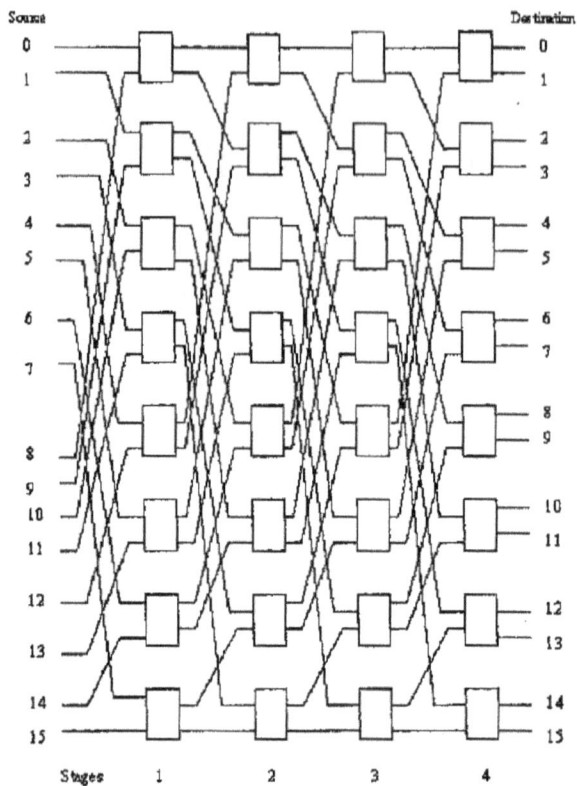

Fig 3.3 Omega Network

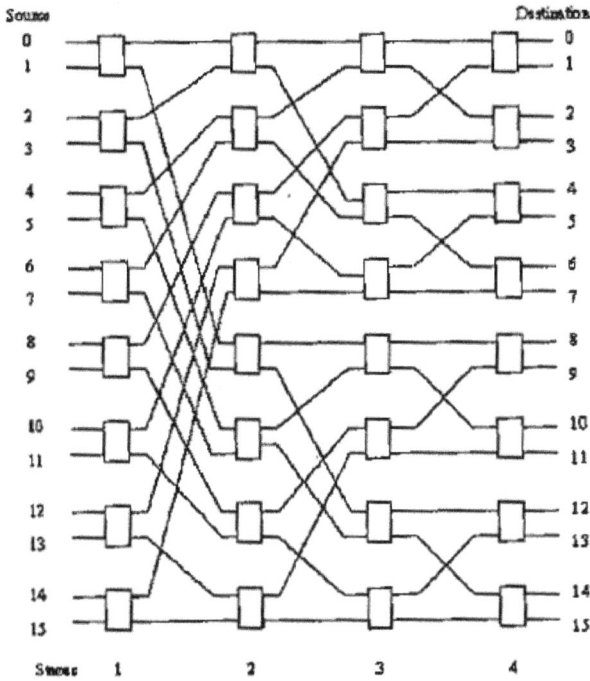

3.3 MULTIPATH NETWORKS

The multipath networks provide more than one path between source-destination pairs. So, if a particular path is faulty or if a particular output link is busy, then the request can be routed through alternate path available. The multipath networks are better than the unique path networks in terms of performance because they allow alternate routing to be possible.

This prevents the disconnection of the source-destination pairs in case of some faults. These multipath networks can be either static or dynamic. In static interconnection networks, the network topology remains the same all the time whereas in dynamic interconnection networks, the path can change from one communication to another. Hence, in static networks data has to backtrack to the source or some fixed point to select an alternative path for routing. But in dynamic networks if a fault is encountered in a particular stage the switching element in preceding stage re-routes the data through an alternate available path.

Moreover, the MINs can be either regular or irregular. Regular MINs have got an equal number of switching elements per stage and as a result they impose equal time delay to all requests passing through them. But irregular MINs have unequal number of switching elements per stage. For a given source-destination pair, there are different path lengths available with shortest path length of 2. So, these networks help in reducing delay when requests pass through shorter paths available.

Hence, for studying these networks different categories can be formed depending on whether they are regular or irregular, static or dynamic.

3.3.1 Multipath Regular Static MINs

As the name suggests, MINs of this category will provide more than one path between source-destination pairs. Moreover, they will contain equal number of switching elements per stage and will have a fixed network topology. Some of the MINs belonging to this category are Extra Stage Cube (ESC) Network [2], and INDRA Network [21].

3.3.1.1 Extra Stage Cube (ESC) Network

ESC network is formed from the Generalized Cube network by adding an extra stage to the input side of the network along with the multiplexers and demultiplexers at the input and output stages respectively. This extra stage provides an additional path from each source to each destination. The Extra Stage Cube network provides complete fault tolerance for any single failure. Fig 3.5 shows Extra Stage Cube network for N=8.

The ESC network is built from the generalized cube network by adding an extra stage m together with some hardware to bypass the interchange boxes of the extra stage and those of stage zero. The interchange boxes of stage m share a common control signal to enable or disable them, which is also true for the interchange boxes in stage zero. The normal operation of the network takes place with stage m disabled and stage 0 enabled. If a fault occurs in stage 0, then the extra stage m is enabled and stage 0 disabled. This helps in providing fault tolerance in the ESC network and there is significant overall gain in the network reliability as a result of this extra stage.

Main features of the network are as follows:

For an N x N ESC network

No. of stages = $\log_2 N + 1$

No. of switches per stage = $N/2$

No. of links/stage = N

3.3.1.2 INDRA Network

Interconnection Networks Designed for Reliable Architectures (INDRA) incorporates union of R parallel copies of a basic unique path network with an initial distribution stage. The stages are numbered from 0 to n from input to output (n = logRN). If the R redundant links to stage 0 are not used, then there exist R paths between source and destination pair. By using the redundant links, there exist R2 paths, though not all disjoint, between source and destination pair. INDRA network is R-1 fault tolerant and is quite reliable in general. Fig 3.6 shows INDRA network .

Main features are of the network are as follows:

For an N x N ESC network

No. of stages = log2N+1

No. of switches per stage = $N/2$

No. of links/stage = N

3.3.2 Multipath Regular Dynamic MINs

The MINs belonging to this category are dynamic that is no backtracking is required in case of a fault as the switching element reroutes data through the alternate available path in the network. Hence, a fork exists at every point in the network for rerouting of data and this helps in reducing the unnecessary delay or latency.

Augmented Shuffle Exchange Network (ASEN) [15], Augmented Baseline Network (ABN) [8], Inverse Augmented Data Manipulator (IADM) [23] and F-network [19] are examples of such types of networks.

3.3.2.1 Augmented Shuffle Exchange Network (ASEN)

ASEN-2 is built on the concept of conjugate SEs. At every stage, there is a subset of conjugate SEs leading to the same set of destinations. And within each conjugate SEs, there exists conjugate pair of switches. These pair of switches is connected to the same SEs in the next stage. Hence the switches belonging to the conjugate subset are connected using additional intrastage links to form loops within the constraint that switches in a loop belong to same conjugate subset and that no two SEs in a loop form a conjugate pair. In case of faulty SE or a faulty loop, its conjugate can replace it without affecting the network performance. Fig 3.7 shows ASEN for N=16.

Multiple paths are achieved in the network by connecting the switches to a conjugate subset by using additional links to form loops. The vertical links that are used to connect switches in the same stage are called auxiliary links. By using these auxiliary links fault-tolerant routing can be accomplished.

If a switch is not able to process a request because of a faulty switch in the next stage or because of a busy output link, it can re-route that request via its auxiliary destination link to the conjugate switch in the loop. The next switch in turn will make connection to a different fault free switch in the following stage. Hence, a switching element in ASEN-2 can detect the failure of its successor SE and reroute the request whenever possible.

An N x N ASEN-2 consists of $\log_2 N$-l number of stages out of which $\log_2 N$-2 stages consist of N/2 SEs per stage of size 3x3 and one stage consists of N/2 SEs of size 2x2.

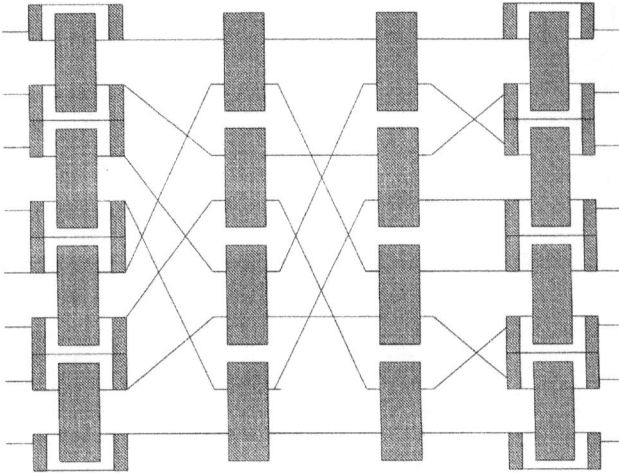

Fig 3.5 Extra Stage Cube (ESC) Network

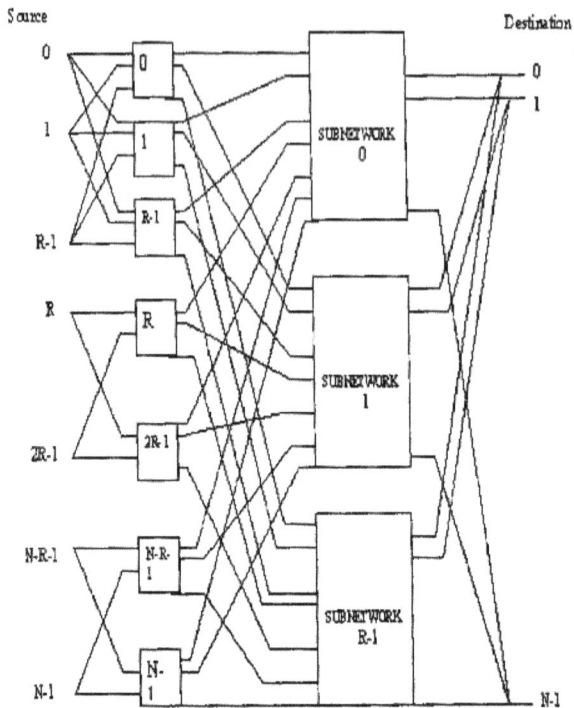

Fig 3.6 INDRA Network

Main features of the network are as follows:

For an N x N ASEN-2 network
No, of stages = $\log_2$ N-l
No. of 2 x 1 multiplexers = N
No. of 1 x 2 demultiplexer = N

3.3.2.2 Augmented Baseline Network (ABN)

An NxN ABN consists of two identical subnetworks, denoted as Gi consisting of N/2

sources and N/2 destinations each. Each group consists of a multiple path, modified baseline network of size N/2. The modified baseline network is a baseline network with one less stage and feature links among the switches belonging to the same stage, forming loops of switches. The switches in the last stage are of size 2x2 and remaining switches in stages from 1 to (n-3), where n=log₂N, are of size 3x3, in each stage, the switches are grouped into conjugate pairs. These conjugate pairs are grouped into conjugate subsets. Multiple path property is achieved by permitting two switches in the same conjugate subset that are not a conjugate pair, to communicate through auxiliary links, to form a loop. Fig 3.8 shows ABN for N=16.

Main features of the network are as follows:

For an N x N ABN network
No. of stages = $\log_2 N - 2$
No. of 4 x 1 multiplexers = N
No. of 1 x 2 demultiplexer = N

3.3.2.3 Inverse Augmented Data Manipulator (IADM)

This class of multistage interconnection networks is based on the PM2I interconnection functions. Each stage consists of N switching elements and there are m stages, where m = $\log_2 N$. At stage i of the network, the first output link of the switching element j is connected to switching element j-2 (modulo N) of stage i-1 (interconnection function PM2-i), the second output link is connected to the switching element j of stage i-1 (straight) and the third output link of the switching element] is connected to switching element J+2 (modulo N) of stage i-1 (interconnection function PM2+i). Hence, these links are termed as MINUS, STRAIGHT and PLUS links. Fig 3.9 shows IADM for N=8.

There are multiple paths available in the IADM network. The available paths between any source (S) and any destination (D) are those satisfying the condition that the sum of the corresponding links equals to D-S modulo N. The existence of multiple paths makes IADM network more fault-tolerant. Also the presence of multiple paths improves the performance and reliability of IADM network over the unique path networks.

Main features of the network are as follows:
For an N x N ABN network
No. of stages = $\log_2 N$
No. of switches per stage = N
No. of links/stage = 3N

3.3.2.4 F-Network

F Network basically adds links to the generalized cube network. At each stage except the output stage, two different switches can be selected while maintaining the same destination. Blocked routes can be avoided by choosing an appropriate path. F network is single fault tolerant and robust in presence of multiple paths. F network is quite reliable but the efficiency degrades drastically for higher network sizes. Fig 3.10 shows F-network for N=8.

F-Network assumes:

- Failure of only internal switches
- Failed switches are unusable
- Faults occur independently

Main features of the network are as follows:
For an N x N F- network
No. of stages = $\log_2 N + 1$
No. of switches per stage = N

3.3.3 Multipath Irregular Static MINs

MINs belonging to this category being static have a fixed network topology. Also there will be unequal number of switching elements in each stage, as these MINs are irregular in nature. In case of fault in such MINs, data will have to be backtracked to the source or some fixed point in order to route the request through an alternate path.

Double Tree (DOT) network [17] and Fault Tolerant Double Tree (FDOT) network [5] are examples of these types of networks.

3.3.3.1 Double Tree Network

This DOT network proposed by Levitt is an irregular type of multistage interconnection network. It consists of a right and left half and is non-fault tolerant. Each half resembles a binary tree, with the left half and right half being the mirror images of each other. A DOT network of size NxN has N sources and N destination terminals. The flip control (i.e. individual stage control) used in the DOT network affects the performance and reliability of the entire system, As the DOT network is irregular, so it has shorter path length for a connection between a processor and its favorite memory module. Fig 3.11 shows DOT network for N=8.

Main features of the network are as follows:

For an N x N DOT network

No. of stages $= 2n-1$ ($n=log_2 N$)

No. of SEs $= 2^{n+1} -3$

Number of SEs in stage i and stage $(2n-i) = 2^{n-i}$

3.3.3.2 Fault Tolerant Modified Double Tree Network (FDOT)

In the FDOT network, different layers of static DOT networks are combined to construct the FDOT network. The irregular FDOT-k network consists of k independent subnetworks of size (N/k * N/k) and an extra one. The extra subnetwork is added to further enhance the fault tolerance and to improve the reliability, FDOT-k is k fault tolerant. As the network is irregular, there exists multiple paths of different path lengths and due to this chances of blocking are also further reduced. And hence the network gives better performance than other MINs, Fig 3.12 shows FDOT network for N = 16.

Main features of the network are as follows:

For an N x N FDOT network

No. of stages $= 2n-1$ ($n=log2N/2$)

No. of SEs $= 3.(2n+1-3)$

No. of 2:1 multiplexers $= 3N/2$

No. of 1:2 demultiplexers $= 3N/2$

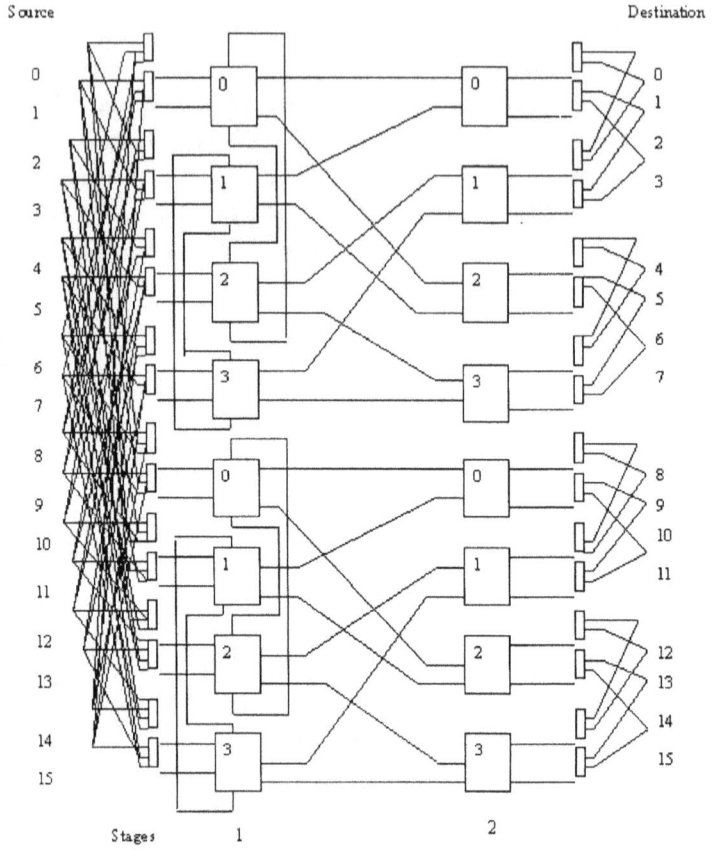

Fig 3.7 Augmented Shuffle Exchange Network (ASEN)

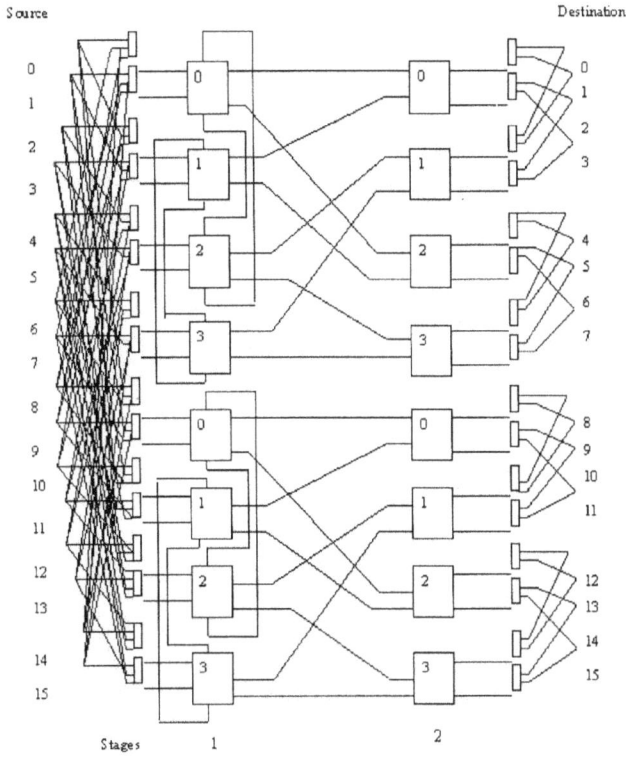

Fig 3.8 Augmented Baseline Network (ABN)

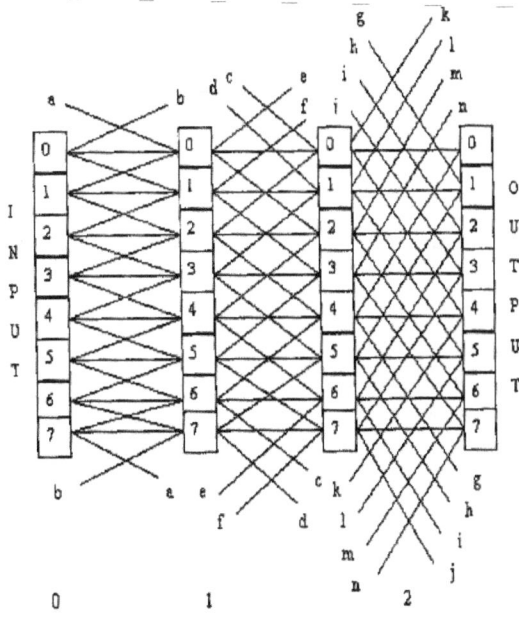

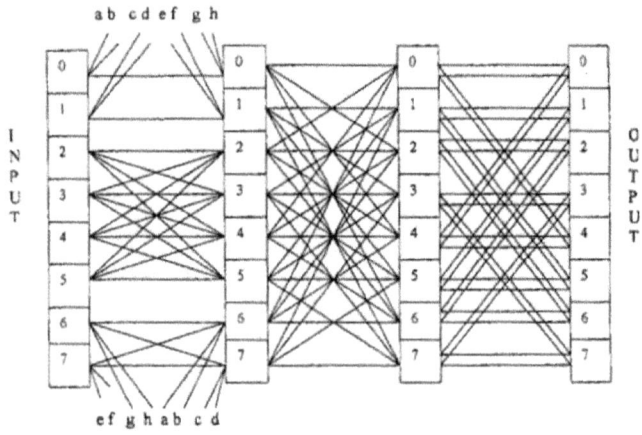

Fig 3.10 F-Network

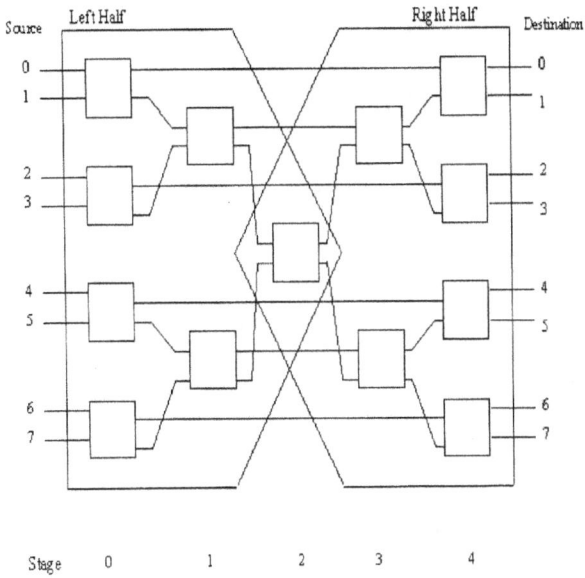

Fig 3.11 Double Tree (DOT) Network

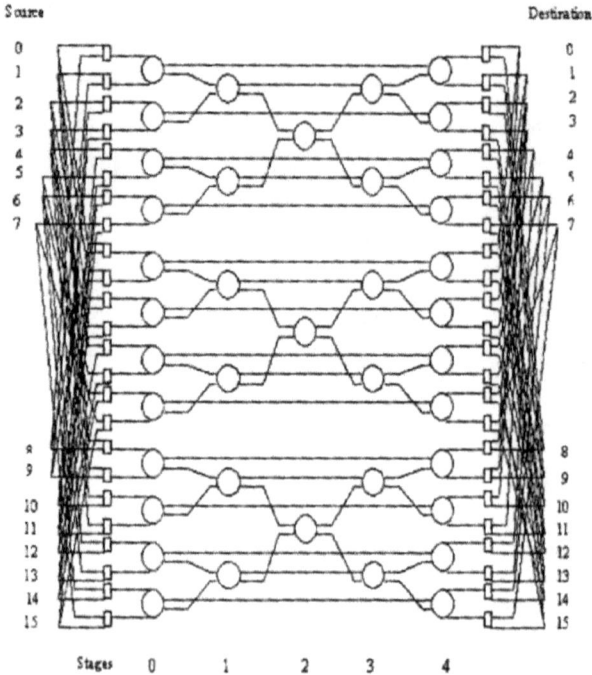

Fig 3.12 Fault-Tolerant Double Tree (FDOT) Network

3.3.4 Multipath Irregular Dynamic MINs

The MINs belonging to this category have unequal number of switching elements at its stages. As these are dynamic no backtracking is required in case of a fault

Four Tree (FT) network [6] is an example of MIN belonging to this category.

3.3.4.1 Four Tree (FT) Network

FT being an irregular Dynamic MIN supports multiple paths of different lengths. It is a dynamically reroutable irregular MIN that has chaining among the switches to enhance the fault tolerance. Full access is provided in case of single fault FT network of size NxN consists of $(2m-1)$ (where $m = \log_2 N/2$) number of stages with $(2^{m+2} - 6)$ of switches; 2^{n-1} (where $n = \log_2 N$) are of size 2x2 and the rest are of size 3x3. It is constructed with the help of two identical groups, each consisting of MDOT network. The two groups are formed based on the most significant bit (MSB) of the source-destination terminals. Thus, half of the source-destination terminals with MSB 0 fall into G^0 group and the others having MSB 1 fall into G^1 group, Both the subgroups are connected by means of the multiplexers and demultiplexers in the first and the last stages to provide the fault tolerance. The switches in a stage having the same number in both the groups form a loop. Such loops are formed in every stage except the last one. Every request generated by the source is first routed through the primary path. If the path is unavailable due fault or if the particular output link is busy, the request is routed through the other secondary subgroup. Fig 3.13 shows FT network for N=1 6.

Main features of the network are as follows:

For an N x N FT network

No. of stages = 2m -1 (where m = $\log_2$N/2)

No. of switches = 2^{m+2} - 6

No. of 2:1 Multiplexers = N

No. of 1:2 Demultiplexers = N

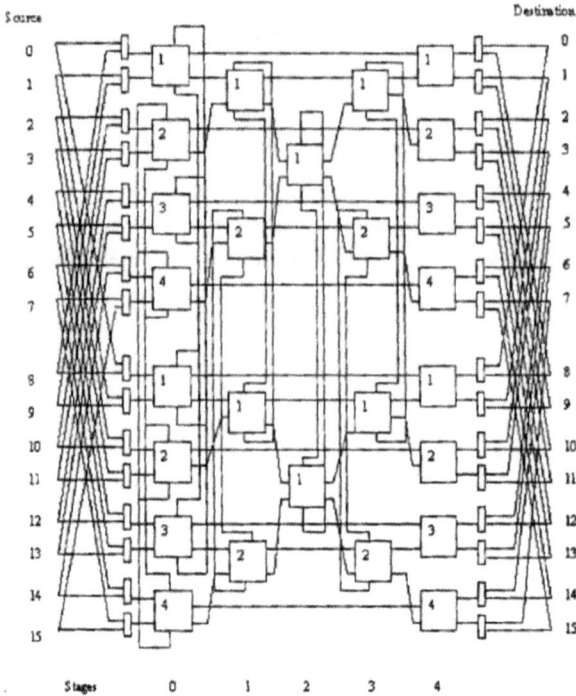

Fig 3.13 Four Tree (FT) Network

3.4 CONCLUSION

This chapter deals with overview of existing unique path, multipath, static, dynamic multistage interconnection networks possessing regular and irregular topologies. It provides full constructional features and is helpful in design of new multistage interconnection networks, It gives an insight on various aspects of multistage interconnection networks so that new networks having better performance can be designed. It also helps to know the various openings in the field in which further work can be carried out.

The next chapter discusses the proposed Irregular, Fault tolerant Irregular Augmented Shuffle Network (IASN).

CHAPTER 4 : IRREGULAR AUGMENTED SHUFFLE NETWORK

4.1 INTRODUCTION

A new class of irregular fault tolerant multistage interconnection network named Irregular Augmented Shuffle Network (IASN) has been proposed and analyzed in this chapter. As the network is irregular, 50% of the requests pass through minimum path length of 2 in comparison to the regular networks, which have a constant path length. Thus, the irregular network IASN helps in reducing the latency or delay. Moreover, the network is fault tolerant i.e. it is capable of serving requests even in presence of certain faults. IASN has been designed in a way to improve the performance of the network, which includes reliability, permutation passability, probability of acceptance and bandwidth. Moreover, the IASN network is cost-effective too.

4.2 CONSTRUCTION PROCEDURE OF IASN

Irregular Augmented Shuffle Network (IASN) of size N x N is constructed of two identical subgroups consisting of N/2 sources and N/2 destinations, denoted as G^i (where i =0,1). The two groups are formed on the basis of most significant bit (MSB) of the source-destination pair. If the MSB of source-destination pair is 0, then it belongs to G^0 group otherwise if MSB is 1, then it belongs to G^1 group. Both the groups are connected to the N sources and N destinations with the help of multiplexers and demultiplexers.

IASN network is an irregular multistage interconnection network, An NxN (2^n x 2^n) network (where N is the number of sources and destinations, n = $\log_2 N$) consists of m stages (where m = $\log_2 N/2$). The first and the last stage of the network consist of equal number of switching elements (SEs) that is 2^{n-1} each whereas the intermediate stages consist of less number of switching elements equal to 2^{n-2} each. The switches in the last stage are of size 2x2 and the rest switches from stage 1 to m-1 are of size 3x3. Thus, the total number of switches are equal to 2^{n-2} (m+2) out of which 2^n number of switches are of size 2x2 and (m-2)x 2^{n-2} number of switches are of size 3x3. There is one 4x1 multiplexer for each input link of a switch in first stage and one 1x2 demultiplexer for each output link of switch in the last stage. Hence, there exists 2N multiplexers and demultiplexers of size 4x1 and 1 x2 respectively.

The network being an irregular network supports multiple paths of varied path lengths. The network is regular in the first and last stage as it consists of same number of switching elements but it is irregular in the intermediate stages, which consist of less number of switching elements. Multiple paths are available for passing requests from a particular source to a particular destination. This makes the network fault-tolerant as requests route through alternate paths available.

At each stage except the last, there exists a fork at every point so that routing from source to destination can take place from an alternate path in presence of faults or when a particular output link if busy. At each stage except the last, the switching elements are linked by auxiliary links to form a loop. These SEs hence form a conjugate loop. So, if a particular switching element is faulty or a particular output link is busy, routing takes place through the use of auxiliary links, which helps in maturing of the requests through the other fault-free SE present in the loop.

Fig 4.1 and Fig 4.2 shows the construction of IASN for size N=16 and its corresponding redundancy graph respectively.

Redundancy graph is a method of showing all possible paths between source and destination pairs. It depicts the various paths available for routing so that if a particular path is faulty, routing can take place through alternate paths available. Redundancy graph of IASN network as shown in Fig 4.2 depicts the various possible paths available in the network.

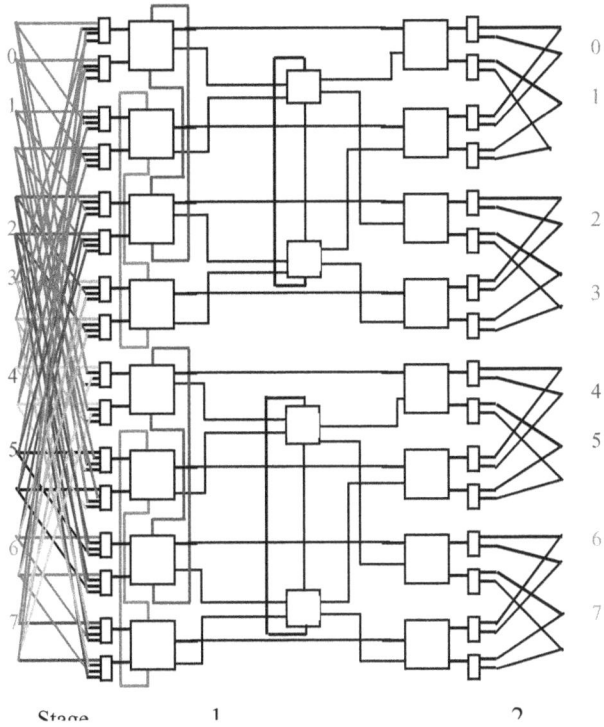

Fig 4.1 Irregular Augmented Shuffle Network (IASN)

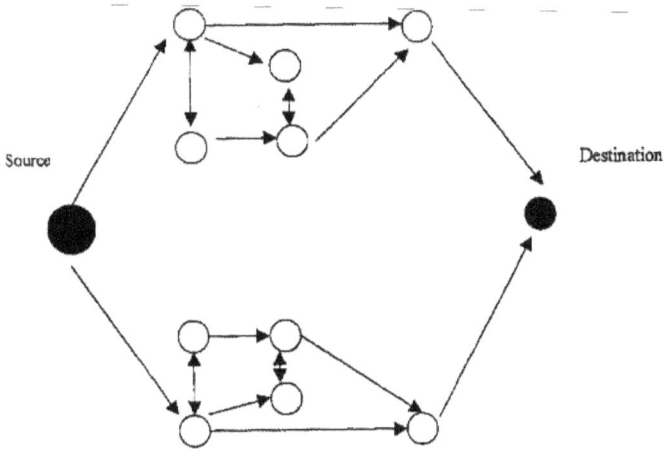

Fig 4.2 Redundancy Graph of IASN

4.3 ROUTING PROCEDURE FOR IASN

Routing tag consists of binary digits that control the connection through different stages

of the path from input to the output.

Let the source S and destination D be represented in binary as:

$$S = s_{n-1}., \ldots \ldots s_1 s_0$$
$$D = d_{n-1}. \ldots \ldots d_1 d_0$$

The routing scheme for IASN is described as follows:

Algorithm: Fault Tolerant Routing for IASN

PROCEDURE

---

i.	One of the networks G^i is selected on the basis of most significant bit (MSB) of the destination address for routing the request to a particular destination.
ii.	For each source-destination pair, there exist two paths called primary and secondary path. Firstly, the request tries to enter through the primary path. If the primary path is faulty, then the secondary path is chosen. And if secondary path is also faulty, then the network fails.
iii.	The routing tag bit is the destination address with its MSB removed. This tag bit determines the path that is chosen for routing a request from source to destination.
iv.	If a particular output link is faulty or the switch in the next stage is faulty, then the request is passed to another switch in the same stage through a third link called auxiliary or express link. If this auxiliary link is also faulty, then the request is dropped.
v.	At the end, for routing the request through the demultiplexer, bit

do of the routing tag is used.

Example

Let the data be routed from S=0000 to various destinations of a 2^4 x2^4 IASN network. The path lengths calculated for set of destinations are as summarized in the Table 4.1.

S	D	Path Lengths available
	0000	
	0001	
	0010	
	0011	2,3
	1000	
	1001	
	1010	
	1011	
	0000	
	0100	
	0101	
	0110	
	0111	3
	1100	
	1101	
	1110	
	1011	

Table 4.1 Routing Information for IASN

4.4 FAULT-TOLERANCE OF IASN

Fault tolerance in an interconnection network is very important for continues operation over relatively long period of time. Fault tolerance is the ability of the system to continue operating in the presence of faults although at a degraded performance [6]. These faults can be either permanent or transient in nature [22]. It is criteria that must be met for a network to operate even in presence of certain faults.

The network should be able to satisfy the criteria of full access that is ability of the network to transfer data from any input terminal to any output terminal. In case of fault-free conditions, one to one connection is maintained and in presence of faults alternate paths are chosen for routing. So, under the criteria of full access a network is assumed to be faulty if there is any input-output pair that cannot be connected with each other due to the presence of faulty components in the network.

A network is single fault tolerant if it can function as specified by its fault tolerance criteria despite any single faults conforming to its fault models. A network is said to be k fault tolerant if it can still provide a connection for any source destination pair in the presence of any instance of upto k faults in the network [26].

The proposed IASN network satisfies the fault tolerance criteria as it can operate even in presence of certain faults. Fault tolerance has been achieved by providing a primary as well as secondary path from source to destination so that if the primary path is faulty, then secondary path can be chosen. Every source-destination pair has a fork available at every stage except at the last one.

A network is robust in the presence of k faults if it can tolerate some instance of k faults. The maximum number of faults it can tolerate comes from the case that only one of the groups is fault-free [26].

The presence of the auxiliary links available in the network provides an alternate path for routing, except at the last stage. But if the switches in the same loop are simultaneously faulty, then it disconnects certain source-destination pairs. Such a fault is termed as 'critical fault'. So as long as the fault is not critical, the network continues to operate even though at degraded performance. Hence, strictly speaking IASN network is single switch fault tolerant.

The multiple paths between S = 0000 and D = 0110 and between S = 0000 and D = 1010 are as shown in Fig 4.3.

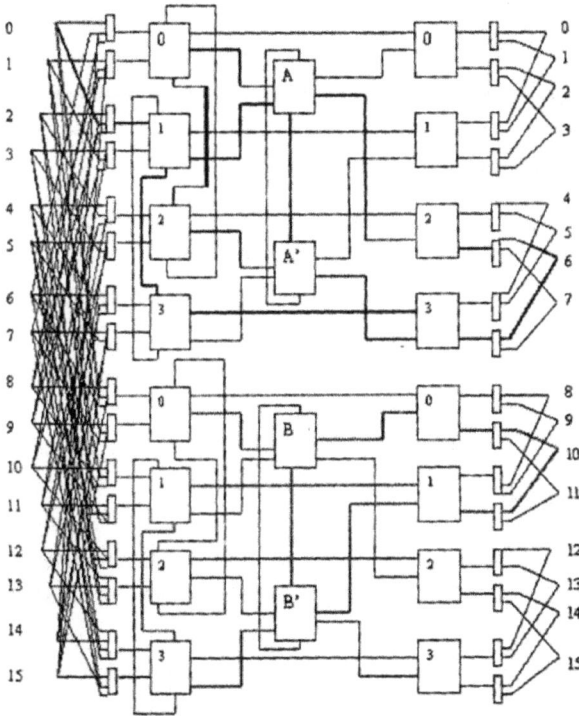

Fig 4.3 IASN highlighting multiple paths between S-D pairs

The following theorems characterize the faults that can be tolerated in the IASN network.

Theorem 1: In IASN network, if the faults occur such that at most one switch is affected in every pair of switches in a loop (that is conjugate switches), then there exists at least one fault-free path from any source to any destination.

Proof : Since there is at most one switch affected in the loop of conjugate switches, the other switch is fault-free. Thus, through the auxiliary or express link, the other fault-free switch can be reached. As both the switches lead to the same destination, so requests instead of getting blocked pass through the fault-free switch in the same loop. Hence, there exists at least one fault-free path from any source to any destination.

Theorem 2: In IASN, some source is disconnected from some destination if both the switches in a loop are simultaneously faulty.

Proof: Suppose that while routing from any source to any destination there exists a faulty switch in the route, The network will try to route the request through another switch in the same loop. But if both the switches are simultaneously faulty, then clearly some sources will be disconnected from certain destinations.

Lemma 1: IASN is single switch fault tolerant in stages from 1 to m-1.

Proof: From stages 1 to m-1, there exists SEs that forms pair through the use of auxiliary links. Some sources will be disconnected from some destinations only if both the switches in the loop are simultaneously faulty. In case of single switch failures, sources are connected to destinations through the other fault-free switch available in the loop. Hence, IASN is single switch fault tolerant network.

4.5 RELIABILITY ANALYSIS OF IASN

There are three fault models adopted to the reliability analysis of the networks:stuck-at fault model, switch-fault model and link-fault model. In the stuck-at fault model, a failure causes a crossbar switch to remain in a particular state regardless of the control inputs given to it, thus affecting its capability to set up suitable connections. In switch fault model, a switch is considered to be totally unusable if it becomes faulty. In the link fault model, a failure affects an individual link of a switch leaving remaining part of the switch operational [4,8,22]. Any network fault that corrupts data on the information path is called a link fault, A link fault occurs in an information link when it becomes stuck at either logical 0 or 1, regardless of the actual input signal applied to it. In this thesis, switch fault model is used for the analysis of the network. It is assumed that any of the switching component i.e. switching elements, multiplexers and demultiplexers can fail in the IASN network. All the faults are assumed to be independent of each other. The reliability is analyzed in terms of MTTF. The MTTF is analyzed by defining a set of critical components, A critical set of components is defined as set of switching components, each from different groups, such that a network failure will occur if all the components become faulty simultaneously [26].

Certain basic steps are used in the analysis of reliability [7]. These are:

I.   First, the elements, subsystem and estimated individual reliability factors
        are identified.

II.   Then a block diagram representing the logical manner in which these elements are
        connected is prepared to form a system.

III   Then the condition for the successful operation of the system is determined that is
        it is decided that how many units should function together.

IV.   Finally the combinational rules of probability theory that is add, multiply
and

        their combinations are applied to arrive at the system reliability factor.

The following assumptions are made during reliability analysis [8] :

Assumptions:

        I. Switch failures occur independently in the network with the failure rate of

            λ (=

            10-6 per h)

        II. Based on the gate count, failure rate of 2 x 2 SE is taken as $\lambda 2 = \lambda$; for a 3
             x 3 SE it is

             $\lambda 3 = 2.5 \lambda$ and λ m= m λ /4 for a m x 1 MUX or λ d (=λ m) for a 1 x m
             DEMUX.

III. 2x2 SEs in the last stage and their associated demultiplexers are taken as

series system with a combined failure rate of $\lambda 2d = 2\lambda$.

4.5.1 Upper Bound Analysis

This presents the optimistic value of the reliability, In this it is assumed that the

network will be operational as long as one of the two multiplexers attached to the

source is operational and as long as a conjugate pair of switch is not faulty [3].

The reliability block diagram for the upper bound is as shown in Fig 4,4 (a) and

the corresponding expression is:

$$R_{UB\text{-}IASN(t)} = \left[1 - \left(1 - e^{-\lambda_m t}\right)^2\right]^{N/2} \cdot \left[1 - \left(1 - e^{-\lambda_3 t}\right)^2\right]^{N/4* + N/8* + ...1} \cdot \left[1 - (1 - e^{-\lambda 2d^t})^2\right]^{N/4}$$

$$MTTF = \int_{0}^{\infty} R_{UB\text{-}IASN}(t)\,dt$$

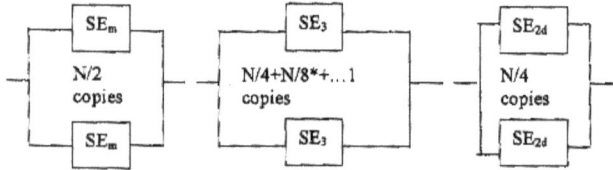

SE$_m$		SE$_3$		SE$_{2d}$
N/2 copies		N/4+N/8*+...1 copies		N/4 copies
SE$_m$		SE$_3$		SE$_{2d}$

Fig 4.4 (a) Upper Bound Reliability Block Diagram

The values for the Upper Bound MTTF for the IASN network are provided in Table 4.2.

Network Size -> PL -	16x16	32x32	64x64	128x128	256x256	512x512	1024x1024
2	155945	105456	72190	49874	34686	24239	16996
3	139275						
4		94419					
5			64769				
6				44816			
7					31203		
8						21822	
9							15311

Table 4.2 Upper Bound MTTF for IASN
The values of upper bound MTTF for other networks like ASEN-2 [15], ABN

Network Size	16x16	32x32	64x64	128x128	256x256	512x512	1024x1024
UB	134935	77685	47339	29855	19255	12611	8353

Table 4.3 Upper Bound MTTF for ASEN-2

Network Size	16x16	32x32	64x64	128x128	256x256	512x512	1024x1024
UB	171627	91329	53434	32884	20867	13511	8872

Table 4.4 Upper Bound MTTF for ABN

Network Size	16x16	32x32	64x64	128x128	256x256	512x512	1024x1024
UB	171627	115276	78546	54084	37525	26178	18334

Table 4.5 Upper Bound MTTF for FT

4.5.2 Lower Bound Analysis

In the lower bound analysis each group is considered independently and it is assumed to be faulty if there is single fault in it. The input side SEs and their associated multiplexers are taken as series system and failure of any component is assumed to be failure of all three. Hence, in this the results are pessimistic in nature.

The reliability block diagram for the lower bound is as shown in Fig 4.4 (b) and the corresponding expression is:

$$R_{\text{LB-IASN}(t)} = \left[1 - \left(1 - e^{-\lambda_{3m}t}\right)^2\right]^{N/4} \left[1 - \left(1 - e^{-\lambda_{3}t}\right)^2\right]^{N/4^* + N/8^* + \dots 1} \cdot \left[1 - \left(1 - e^{-\lambda_{2d}t}\right)^2\right]^{N/4}$$

$$MTTF = \int_{0}^{\infty} R_{\text{LB-IASN}}(t)\,dt$$

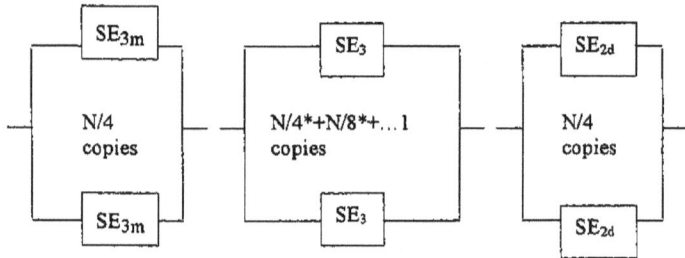

Fig 4.4 (b) Lower Bound Reliability Block Diagram

The values for the Lower Bound MTTF for the IASN network are provided in Table 4.6.

Network Size -> / PL -	16x16	32x32	64x64	128x128	256x256	512x512	1024x1024
2	117465	78067	52778	36133	24966	17364	12135
3	102088						
4		68559					
5			46704				
6				32150			
7					22301		
8						15554	
9							11191

Table 4.6 Lower Bound MTTF for IASN

Network Size	16x16	32x32	64x64	128x128	256x256	512x512	1024x1024
UB	110383	69950	43375	27700	18035	11900	7928

Table 4.7 Lower Bound MTTF for ASEN-2

Network Size	16x16	32x32	64x64	128x128	256x256	512x512	1024x1024
UB	94872	53944	32667	20546	13241	8676	5752

Table 4.8 Lower Bound MTTF for ABN

Network Size	16x16	32x32	64x64	128x128	256x256	512x512	1024x1024
UB	142743	95166	64500	44244	30613	21315	14907

Table 4.9 Lower Bound MTTF for FT

The values of lower bound MTTF for other networks like ASEN-2 [15], ABN [8]

and FT [6] network are given in Table 4.7, 4.8 and 4.9 respectively.

Fig 4.5(a) and Fig 4.5(b) shows the comparative Upper Bound MTTF and Lower Bound MTTF analysis of IASN with regular ASEN-2 and ABN networks respectively.

Fig 4.5(c) and Fig 4.5(d) shows the comparative Upper Bound MTTF and Lower Bound MTTF analysis of IASN with irregular FT network respectively.

From Fig 4.5(a) it can be seen that the Upper Bound MTTF of AJSN is comparable to ASEN-2 and ABN for small network sizes but as the network size increases, the MTTF of IASN is better than ASEN-2 as well as ABN. Also from Fig 4.5(c) it can be seen that the Upper Bound MTTF of IASN slightly less than FT network for small network sizes but becomes comparable as the size increases. This implies that IASN is more reliable in comparison to ASEN-2 and ABN network and is comparable with the FT network.

From Fig 4.5(b) it can be seen that the Lower Bound MTTF of IASN is comparable to ASEN-2 but greater than ABN for small network sizes but as the network size increases, the MTTF of IASN is better than both ASEN-2 as well as ABN. Also from Fig 4.5(d) it can be seen that the Lower Bound MTTF of IASN is less than FT network for small network sizes but becomes comparable as large network sizes. This implies that IASN is more reliable in comparison to ASEN-2 and ABN network. IASN is less reliable than FT network for small network sizes and is comparable with FT network for very large network sizes.

Upper bound MTTF for minimum path length

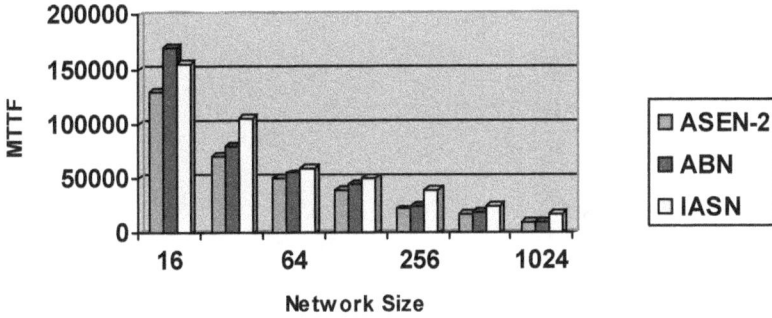

Fig 4.5(a) Comparative Analysis of Upper Bound MTTF

Lower bound MTTF for minimum path length

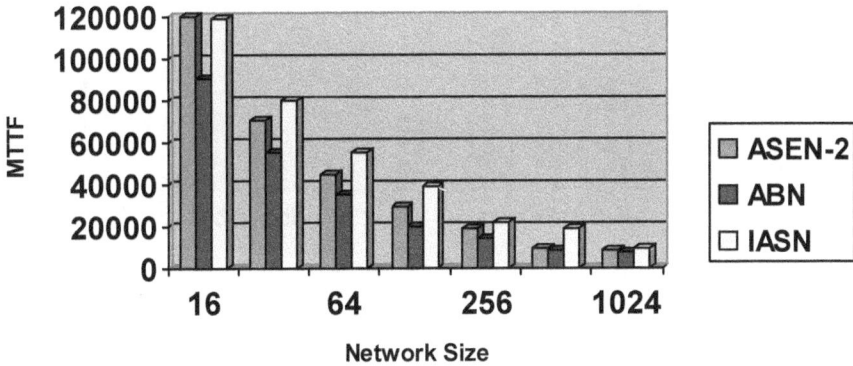

Fig 4.5(b)   Comparative Analysis of Lower Bound MTTF

Upper bound MTTF for minimum path length

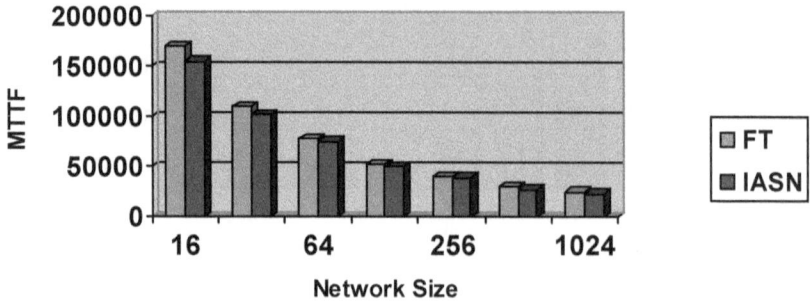

Fig 4.5(c) Comparative Analysis of Upper Bound MTTF

Lower bound MTTF for minimum path length

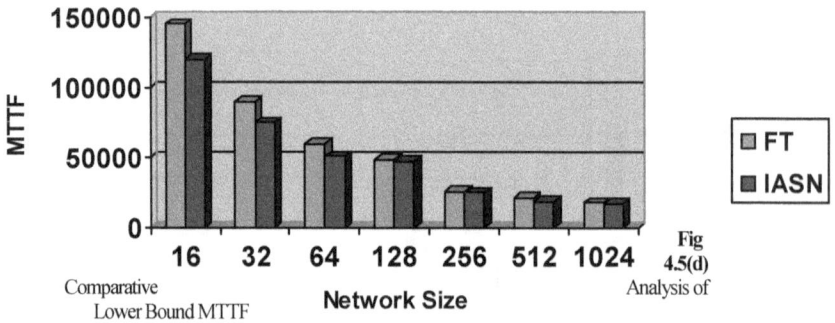

Comparative Lower Bound MTTF

Fig 4.5(d) Analysis of

4.6 PERFORMANCE ANALYSIS OF IASN

The analytical model has been applied to the IASN for evaluating the performance of IASN. The performance parameters that have been analyzed are Bandwidth (BW), Probability of Acceptance (P_a), Throughput (TP), Processor Utilization (PU) and Processing Power (PP).

In IASN, the input and output stages have N/2 SEs each whereas the intermediate stages have N/4 SEs each, Probability of request reaching the final stage will depend on the route taken by the packet to reach the destination. When the request reaches the final stage directly, the path length is 2. But when it passes through the intermediate stages, the maximum path length is $\log_2(N/2)$. For 16 x 16 IASN, a=b=2 and n=4. The bandwidth can be computed as :

$$BW = b^n \, p_n = (2^n \, p_n)/4 + (2^n \, p_{n-3})/8$$

p_n are calculated as:

$$P_n = 1 - [(1-p_{n-1}/2)(1-p_{n-3}/2)]$$

$$P_{n-1} = 1 - [(1-p_{n-2}/2)(1-p_{n-3}/2)]$$

$$p_{n-2} = 1 - (1-p_{n-3})^2$$

$$p_{n-3} = 1 - (1-p_{n-4}/2)^2$$

and   po = p

where p is the memory request rate and it varies over different paths having different

path

lengths.

The probability of acceptance is given by;

$$P_a = BW/a^n p = p_n/4p + p_{n-3}/8p$$

Processor Utilization:

$$PU = p_n/4pT + p_{n-3}/8pT$$

where T is the average time taken.

Processing Power:

$$PP = 2^n \times PU = (2^n p_n)/4pT + (2^n p_{n-3})/8pT$$

Throughput

$$TP = PU \times p = p_n/4T + p_{n-3}/8T$$

The various parameters have been computed and the results are as listed in Table

Request Gen. Prob.	BW	Pa	PU	PP	TP
0.1	0.7306	0.4566	L 0.1826	2.9920	0.01826
0.2	1.3425	0.4195	0.1678	2.6840	0.03356
0.3	1.8602	0.3875	0.1550	2.4800	0.04650
0.4	2.3028	0.3598	0.1439	2.3027	0.05757
0.5	2.6848	0.3356	0.1342	2.1478	0.06712
0.6	3.0172	0.3143	0.1257	2.0114	0.07543
0.7	3.3085	0.2954	0.1181	1.8905	0.08271
0.8	3.5648	0.2785	0.1114	1.7820	0.08910
0.9	3.7910	0.2633	0.1053	1.6848	0.09470
1.0	3.9906	0.2494	0.0990	1.5962	0.09976

4.10.

Table 4.10   Performance Parameters of IASN for N=16

From the above Table 4.10, it can be seen that as the request generation probability increases, bandwidth and throughput increase as more number of packets are delivered to the destination. The probability of acceptance, processor utilization and processing power decrease as the contention among the switches increases.

The performance of IASN has been compared with irregular ALN [22] and PHN [22] networks. The average time taken to route a packet between a source-destination pair is 3.5 for ALN, 3.0 for PHN and 2.5 clock pulses for IASN.

Pa Analysis

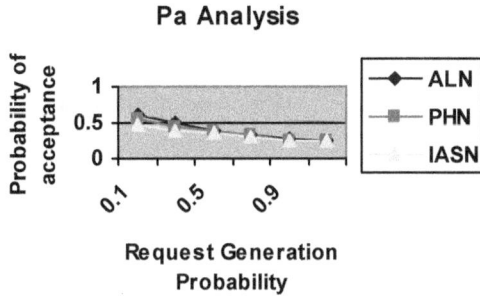

Fig 4.6 (a) Comparative Probability of acceptance

Bandwidth Analysis

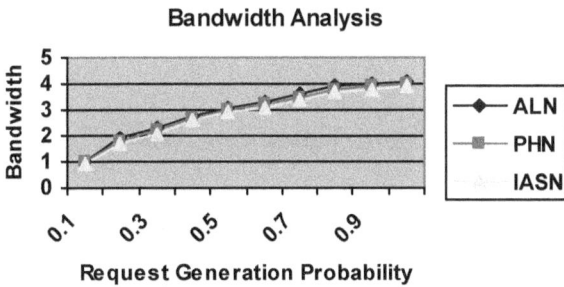

Fig 4.6(b) Comparative   Bandwidth

TP Analysis

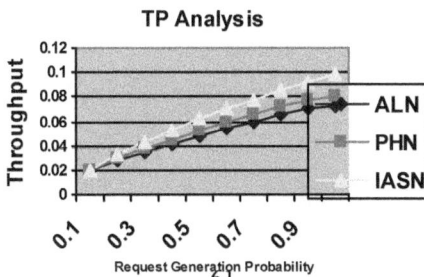

Fig 4.6(c) Comparative Throughput

PU Analysis

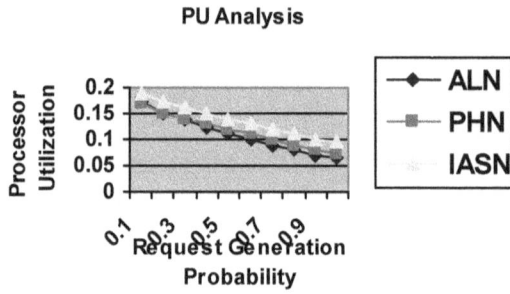

Fig 4.6(d) Comparative Processor utilization

PP Analysis

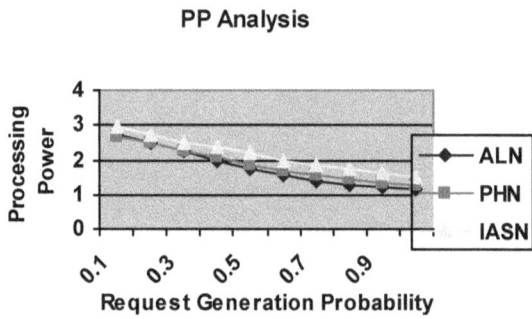

Fig 4.6(e) Comparative Processing Power

Fig 4.6 (a), 4.6 (b), 4.6 (c), 4.6 (d) and 4.6 (e) show the comparative probability of acceptance, bandwidth, throughput, processor utilization and processing power respectively.

From Fig 4.6 (a) and 4.6 (b), it can be seen that probability of acceptance and bandwidth is comparable to the ALN and PHN networks. From Fig 4.6 (c), it can be seen that IASN has considerably high throughput over ALN and PHN as more packets are delivered per unit cycle in IASN. The processor utilization and processing power analysis as depicted in Fig 4.6 (d) and 4.6 (e) also show considerable improvement of IASN over ALN and PHN.

It has been shown in [22] that ALN and PHN have considerable gain in overall performance as compared to FT network. IASN has shown considerable improvement over ALN and PHN and hence, it clearly shows the superiority of IASN over FT network. Moreover, it has been shown that multipath regular ASEN-2 has marginally higher performance than ALN and PHN. Hence, ASEN-2 has higher performance than IASN. But the high performance of ASEN-2 comes at expense of high cost and low reliability. IASN, being an irregular network, has less cost as compared to the regular ASEN. The cost-effectiveness of IASN has been shown in the next section. Hence, by considering all the factors, IASN shows overall gain in performance.

4.7 COST EFFECTIVENESS

The cost of the network also plays a very important role in the evaluation of the network. The network while satisfying other criteria should be cost-effective too. This is because if the increase in performance and reliability of the network also increases the cost of the network, then the network may have a little value in practice.

To estimate the cost of the network, one common method is to calculate the switch complexity with the assumption that cost of the switch is proportional to the number of gates involved, which is roughly proportional to the number of 'cross points' within a switch [20,27]. An mxm switch has m^2 units of cost and it is assumed that each of mx1 multiplexers or 1 x m demultiplexers has m units of cost.

Thus, the cost of the network comes out to be $N/4[32+9\log_2(N/2)]$. To evaluate and compare the cost-effectiveness of the network, the comparison of the cost functions of various networks has been done as shown in Table 4.11.

Table 4.11 Comparative Cost Analysis of related MINs

Networks	Cost Values For Different Network Sizes						
	N=16	N=32	N=64	N=128	N=256	N=S12	N=1024
IASN	236	544	1232	2752	6080	13312	28928
ASEN-2	240	624	1536	3648	8448	19200	43008
ABN	200	544	1376	3328	7808	17920	40448
FT	258	570	1194	2442	4938	9930	19914
ESC	288	640	1408	3072	6656	14336	30720
INDRA	320	768	1792	4096	9216	20480	45056

Fig 4.7(a) and Fig 4.7(b) depicts the cost comparison of IASN with different MINs for small and large network sizes respectively. And it can be depicted that the cost of the proposed AJSN is comparatively less than the regular networks. The cost of IASN comes out to be less than cost of ASEN-2 [15], ABN [8], ESC [2] and INDRA [21] networks. This is due to the irregularity of the network due to which it has less number of switching elements at its intermediate stages.

The cost of IASN is comparable to the irregular FT [6] network at small network sizes but it increases as the network size increases. This is because the IASN network, although being irregular, is regular in the intermediate stages.

Cost Analysis

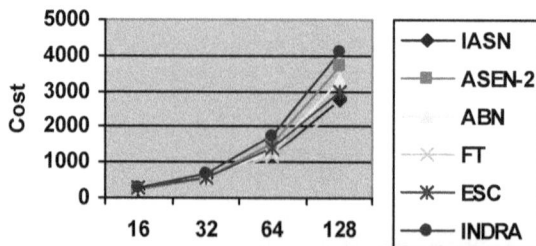

Fig 4.7(a) Comparative Cost Analysis of M'INs

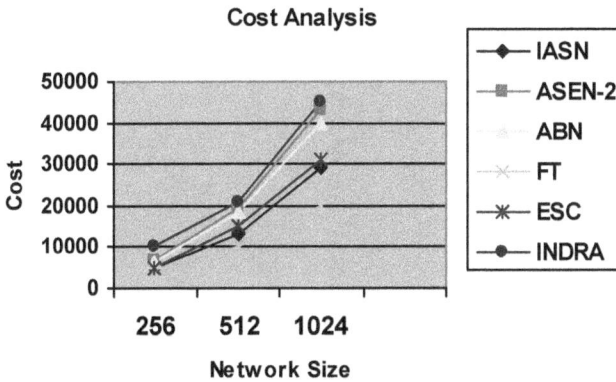

Fig 4.7(b) Comparative Cost Analysis of MINs

4.8 CONCLUSION

A fault-tolerant, irregular multistage interconnection network named Irregular Augmented Shuffle Network (IASN) has been proposed. The network possesses fault tolerance capability and hence operates even under presence of faults. It has reduced number of stages thereby exhibiting reduced latency and better performance.

The reliability analysis, both in terms of upper bound as well as lower bound, shows that IASN is more reliable as compared to existing networks like ASEN-2 and ABN. Moreover, the reliability of IASN is comparable to the existing irregular FT network. The performance analysis also shows overall gain in performance of IASN as compared to various existing networks. Being irregular, IASN is very cost-effective too in comparison to various existing networks like ASEN-2, ABN, INDRA and ESC networks making it a suitable candidate to be used in parallel systems.

The next chapter covers the permutation passability in IASN.

CHAPTER 5	PERMUTATION PASSABILITY IN IASN

5.1 INTRODUCTION

A one-to-one correspondence between source to destination is called permutation. In unique path interconnection networks, there exists only a single path between a source and a destination. But multipath MINs provide various paths between source and destination. When a request occurs, it is first tried through the favorable path i.e. path of minimum length. If that path is unavailable due to:

- Faulty switching elements in the path

- Busy output link

then the request is routed through an alternative path. If no alternative path is available, then the request is simply dropped.

The desirable character of a network is that it should allow maximum requests at minimum path length. Permutation is an important performance consideration for MINs [28].

The source and destination can be represented as:

$$S_i \text{ (where } i = 0,1...N-1)$$

$$D_i \text{ (where } i = 0,1...N-1)$$

Two possible

permutation layouts are

as follows:

- **Identity**

permutations

A one-to-one correspondence between sources Si (I=0,1...N-l) and destinations Di (I=0,1 ...N-l) is called identity permutation and is expressed by:

$$Si = Di \quad \text{for } i=0,1,2......N-1$$

For example: Layout for identity permutations for a network of size=16 can be represented as shown in Fig 5.1.

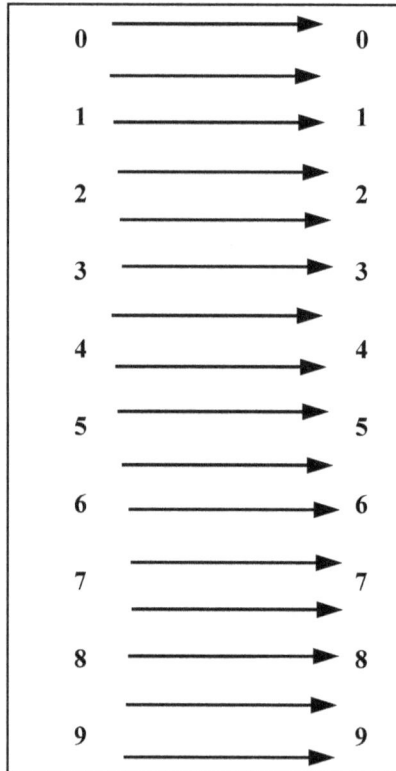

Fig 5.1 Identity Permutations for network of size N -16

Incremental Permutations

Incremental permutation means that each source is connected to the destination in a circular chain.

For example: One possible layout for incremental permutations for a network of size=16 can be represented as shown in Fig 5.2

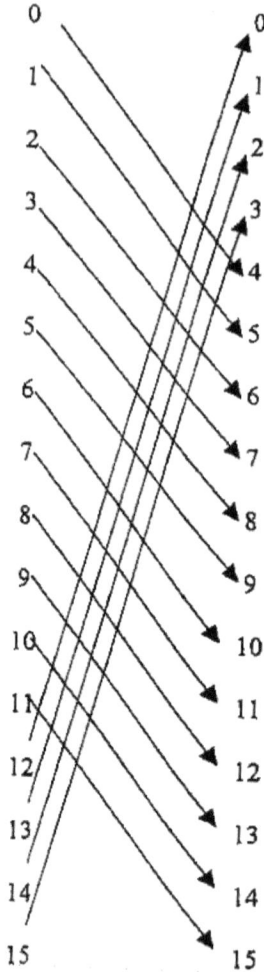

Fig 5.2 Incremental Permutations for network of size N=16

5.2 PERMUTATIONS

To find the identity and incremental permutations for a network, it is assumed that:

X denotes the switches in a non-critical case (if fault is present in a single switch)

Y denotes the switches in a critical case (if switches are faulty in a loop)

PL denotes the path length available in a network. SEs at the i stage are represented as S0, S1... Sn. The multiplexers and demultiplexers are considered as MUX and DEMUX respectively. The probability of issuing a request is 1.0.

5.2.1 Identity and Incremental Permutation Layouts for IASN

The permutation passability of IASN has been evaluated, Table 5.1 and Table 5.2 depict the identity and incremental permutation layouts for IASN respectively. It lists the effect of permutations passed during presence of faults in any component of IASN i.e. multiplexer, SE in any stage i (Si) or demultiplexer.

Faults --> PL	MUX		SO		SI		S2		DEMUX	
	X	Y	X	Y	X	Y	X	Y	X	Y
2	.50	.43	.43	.37	.50	.50	.43	.37	.50	.43
3	.50	.43	.43	.37	.37	.12	.43	.37	.50	.43

Table 5.1 Identity Permutation Layout for IASN

Faults -> PL	MUX		SO		SI		S2		DEMUX	
	X	Y	X	Y	X	Y	X	Y	X	Y
2	0	0	0	0	0	0	0	1 °	0	0
3	.25	.25	.18	.12	.18	.12	.18	.12	.25	,25

Table 5.2 Incremental Permutation Layout for IASN

The percentage of requests passed has been depicted in Fig 5.3(a) and 5.3(b) showing the identity and incremental permutation layout for AISN. It can be seen that in case of identity permutations about 50% of the requests pass through minimum path length of 2 even under presence of faults and the rest pass through the path length of 3.

In case of incremental permutations, none of the permutations pass through minimum path length and only pass through path length of 3.

The results obtained have been compared with existing network like ASEN, ABN and FT network [22]. ASEN-2 and ABN network being regular have a constant path length and the results are depicted in Fig 5.4 and 5.5. FT network being an irregular network has varied path length of 2, 4 and 5. The identity and incremental permutations of FT network are depicted in Fig 5.6(a) and 5.6(b) respectively.

It can be observed that IASN is superior in comparison to ASEN-2 and ABN network, Though ASEN-2 and ABN pass more permutations, they are expensive solution and moreover, being regular they have a fixed path length. Hence, all the requests pass through a fixed path length, which increases the latency as the network size increases.

The results also depict the superiority of IASN over FT network. More identity permutations pass through IASN than FT network. In FT network, no request in passed if a critical fault occurs in the middle stage. But IASN allows certain percentage of requests to be passed even in case of critical faults in any stage. Though IASN and FT network support varied path lengths, the path length of IASN for a given network size is less than that of FT network. This helps in reducing the latency.

Identity Permutation Layout for IASN

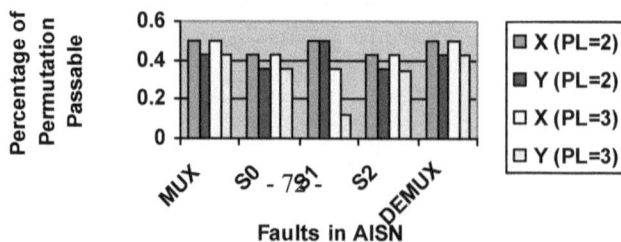

Fig 5.3(a) Identity Permutations Passable in IASN

Incremental Permutation Layout for IASN

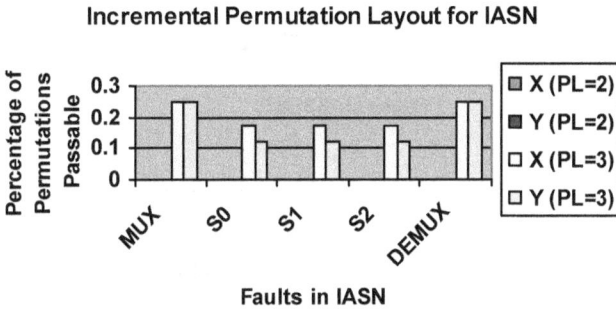

Fig 5.3(b) Incremental Permutations Passable in IASN

5.3 PERMUTATIONS PASSABLE IN OTHER SIMILAR MINs

Permutation Layout for ASEN-2

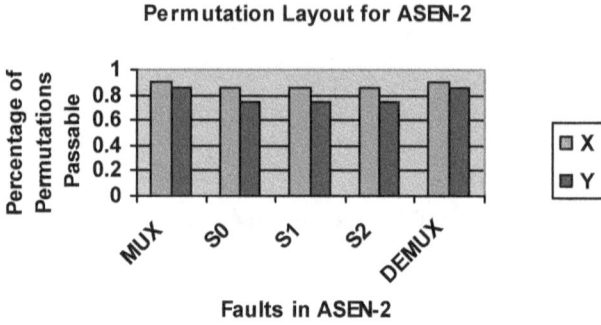

Fig 5,4 Permutations Passable in ASEN-2

Permutation Layout for ABN

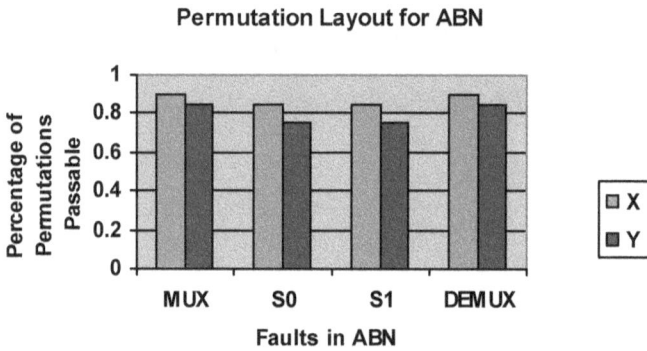

Fig 5.5 Permutations Passable in ABN

Identity Permutation Layout for FT Network

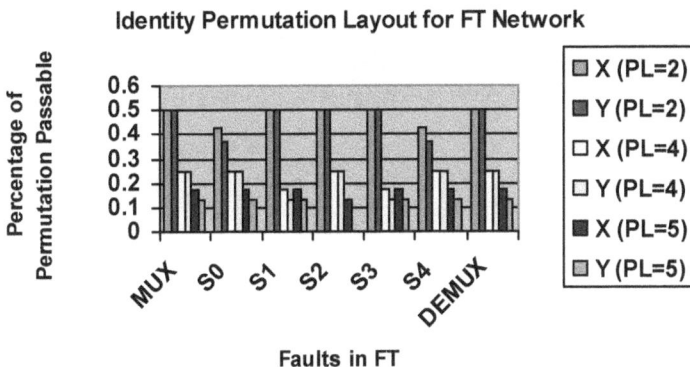

Fig 5.6 (a) Identity Permutations Passable in FT Network

Incremental Permutation Layout for FT Network

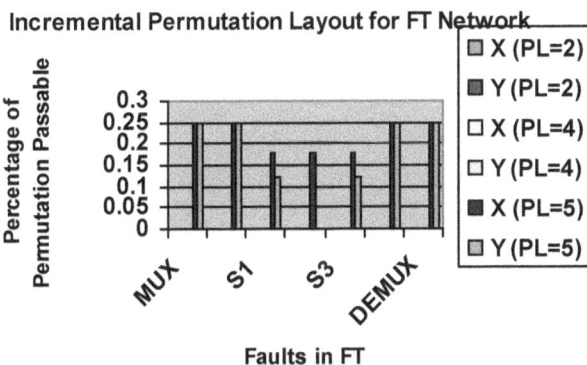

Fig 5.6(b) Incremental Permutations Passable in FT Network

5.4 CONCLUSION

The permutation passability of the proposed IASN has been evaluated and analyzed. The results have been compared with the existing networks like ASEN-2, ABN and FT network. The comparison clearly shows the superiority of IASN over ASEN-2, ABN and FT network.

IASN being irregular passes about 50% of the requests through minimum path length whereas ASEN-2 and ABN being regular have fixed path length and are an expensive solution . Moreover, IASN passes more identity permutations than FT network. It has less path length than FT network, which reduces the latency. Hence, IASN is superior in comparison to regular ASEN-2 &ABN as well as irregular FT network.

CHAPTER 6 FAULT-TOLERANT ROUTING IN MULTISTAGE
INTERCONNECTION NETWORKS

6.1. Introduction

Two pass routing scheme is described for communication in a multiprocessor system employing a unique-path multistage interconnection network in the presence of faults in the network. It is capable of tolerating all single faults and many multiple faults in all except the first and last stages of the network. The routing scheme is useful for tolerating both permanent as well as intermittent faults in the network. The hardware over head for implementing the scheme is very small and no time-penalty is paid in the fault-free case.

.The unique-path property of a MIN facilitates the use of simple routing algorithms for setting up connections through the network. However, the presence of a single fault among the switching elements or the connecting links of these networks destroys the full access property. The effect of such faults cannot be ignored in large systems because of the large number of components involved. Hence, some mechanism for tolerating faults in the networks is important.

The basic idea is to route the data to an incorrect destination in the event that the path to the correct destination is faulty; the data are then routed to the correct destination in a second pass through the network. This is similar to the rerouting schemes used in static interconnection networks [10]. A MIN is said to possess dynamic full access (DFA) capability if every processor in the system can communicate with every other processor in a finite number of passes through the network [9, 11]. Fundamental to our scheme is the observation that a large number of faults do not destroy the DFA capability of a unique-path MIN [11]. Thus, by devising a routing procedure that allows routing through intermediate processors, reconfiguration without the loss of any processor is possible if the faults do not destroy the DFA property of the network. The reconfigured system still operates in a degraded mode owing to the increased latency and the congestion introduced by the loss of paths. However, a large waste of computational effort and resources is prevented.

6.2. Routing

We will describe our routing scheme with respect to an omega network with N =2n ports and n stages of 2 x 2 switching elements. Such a network for N = 16 is shown in Fig. 1. Each processor in the system, with an associated memory unit, forms a processor-memory element (PME). The network stages are numbered 1 to n from left to right. When the network is fault-free, any processor in the system can access the memory unit associated with any of the PMEs in one pass through the network.

We consider a packet-switched network. Routing in the network is achieved by a distributed tag-based scheme. Under this scheme, each message is provided with a header that contains a routing tag. The routing tag is an n-bit binary number which represents the address of the destination port. Routing the message can then be done in a purely distributed manner, with each stage using one of the bits in the routing tag. Specifically, a switching element in stage i of the network looks at bit i of the routing tag; the message is routed to the top output of the switch if this bit is 0 and the bottom output if this bit is 1. Additionally, the header of each message usually contains the address of the source so that an acknowledgement can be sent. Actual transfer of data between stages is accomplished by means of a request acknowledgement handshake protocol.

Faults in the network can affect the switching elements or the interconnecting links or both. Most faults cause failure of the handshake protocol such that data cannot be transferred to a switching element from the preceding switching element in a switching path. Thus the fault is detected by the predecessor. Obviously, not all faults cause a failure of the protocol and such faults are not addressed by this scheme. Alternately, the switching elements can be designed to perform self-tests periodically and signal to the preceding element if a fault is detected. We also exclude faults in the first and last stages of the network and the associated connection links. These parts form the "hard core" of the system. Faults in these stages can be tolerated only by introducing redundant links from the PMEs to the network.

Basically it is a two-pass routing scheme in which a message from the source is routed to a destination (to be referred to as the intermediate destination) different from that specified in the header such that a faulty component in the network is avoided; the intermediate destination then sends the message through the network to the correct destination by making a second pass. The intermediate destination is to be selected such that faulty components in the network are not used during both the passes. Our scheme guarantees this condition for all single faults and many multiple faults in the network.

Working : Let us assume that some switch at position A in stage i $(1 \leq i \leq n - 2)$ finds that it cannot route the message to one of its successors in stage i + 1, say the switching element B. This may be because of a fault in the switching element B or in the connecting link from A to B. Let A1A2...An-1 be the binary representation of A. Then B will be of the form A2A3...An-1A'1. A packet from source s = s1s2...sn to destination d = d1d2...dn will normally be blocked by this fault if

Si + 2si + 3... snd1 ... di = A2A3 ... An-1A'1.   (1)

In our scheme, a message affected by the fault is sent during the first pass to the intermediate destination d' = d'1d'2...d'n, where the individual bits d'1 to d'n are given by

$$
\begin{aligned}
d_j^{'} &= d_j, \quad 1 \leq j \leq i-1; \\
d_i^{'} &= \overline{d}_i; \\
d_{i+1}^{'} &= s_{i+1} or \overline{s}i+1; \\
d_{i+2}^{'} &= \overline{s}i+2; \\
d_j^{'} &= s_j or \overline{s}j, \quad i+3 \leq j \leq n.
\end{aligned}
$$

(2)

This means no change in the route until stage i and using the complement of the routing bit di at stage i. For state i+2 , the complement of the corresponding source bit is used. For the rest of the stages, either the corresponding source address bit or its complement is used as the routing bit instead of the destination bit.

During the second pass, the message is routed from the intermediate destination d' to the final destination d using the original routing tag d1 d2 ... dn.

Before we discuss the implementation of the scheme, we will show that all single faults are tolerated by the scheme. It is easy to see that the faulty component is avoided in the first pass by using the complement of di to route from stage i to i+1. It can also be seen from (1) that the unique path from d' to d does not pass through the switching element or any of its associated links.

87

An example of this scheme is shown in Fig. 1 where the path from input port 7 (0111) to output port 13 (1101) is blocked by a fault in switching element 7 in stage 3. In this case, following (2), either 1000 or 1010 can be used as the routing tag for the first pass. This results in the message being routed to the intermediate destination 8 or 10. The second pass uses the address of the correct destination, that is, 13. It may be verified that the faulty switch is not used in either of the passes.

6.3. Implementation of the scheme

The above scheme can be implemented in a truly distributed manner without the need to compute the routing tag based on the location of the fault. The implementation requires the following:

(1)   An extra routing bit in the header of the message to indicate a misrouted message, called the reroute bit.

(2)   Hardware in the switching elements to read or set the reroute bit and change the routing decision based on this bit.

(3)   Hardware in the PMEs to look at the reroute bit and send the message back to the network if tit is set.

The mechanism works as follows. If a switching element finds that it is unable to send a message to its successor indicated by the routing tag because of a fault, it sets the reroute bit in the header. It then routes the message through the other outgoing link. This has the effect of using the complement of the bit in the routing tag for that stage. Every subsequent switching element receiving the message sees the reroute bit set; instead of using a bit in the destination address for routing, it then uses the complement of the corresponding bit in the source address to route the message. This results in the message being routed to an intermediate destination satisfying (2).

On reaching the intermediate destination, the PME finds the reroute bit of the message set. It then resets this bit and sends the message to the network again, without disturbing the source and destination addresses in the header. The message then makes its way to the proper destination in the second pass, without being blocked by the fault that was encountered in the first pass. Since the source address is not modified, the PME receiving the message can properly identify where to send the acknowledgement. The PMEs do not need to know the location of the fault.

The same mechanism can be applied if more than one fault is present. Some combination of faults cause the message to be rerouted infinitely in the network. Hence, some mechanism should be provided to issue a time-out interrupt if an acknowledgement for a message is not received within a reasonable time interval. A repair needs to be carried out in such a case. Alternately, the first instance of a rerouting can be used to signal a fault; this causes a repair to be scheduled at the next available time. The system mean while operates in the degraded mode until the fault is actually repaired.

The scheme also handles intermittent faults. Rerouting is initiated at the first occurrence of a fault. To ensure that packets are not received out of order it is necessary that all the subsequent messages through the switching element be rerouted as well. However, diagnostics can be run periodically and normal operation can be restored if the fault disappears.

6.4. Conclusion

In this thesis we described a scheme for routing messages in a multistage network in the presence of faults. Its main merit is the low cost associated with its implementation and no loss of performance under normal operation. Faults in the network cause increased latency and blocking, but the connectivity of the system is not affected for any set of tolerable faults.

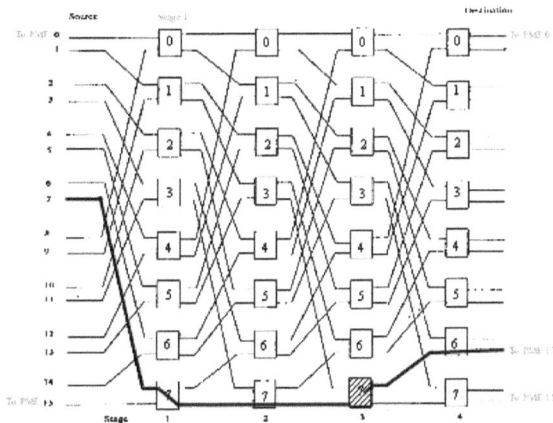

Fig: 6.1 A multiprocessor system interconnected by the omega

CHAPTER 7 ZETA MULTI-STAGE INTERCONNECTION NETWORK

7.1 Introduction

A new class of irregular fault tolerant multistage interconnection network called the ZT Network has been proposed and analyzed in this chapter. As we will see ZT Network can achieve general goals for the design of a fault tolerant network i.e. good performance even in the presence of faults, high reliability, low cost, all permutation passable, and a simple control scheme. In this irregular network 50% of requests are accepted at minimum path length of 2 in contrast with the regular ASEN-2 [14], ESC [2], ABN [6], and Banyan has constant path length on all the routes, which makes delay encountered to the same delay along all the paths, thus increasing average latency.

7.2 Construction procedure of ZETA (ZT) Network

A ZT Network of size N x N is constructed with two identical groups of SEs i.e. G^N, [where $(N = 0,1)$], which are arranged one above the other. The two groups are formed based on the most significant bit (MSB) of the source-destination terminals. Thus half of the source-destination terminals with MSB 0 fall in to the G^0 group and the others having MSB 1 fall into G'. Each source and destination is connected to both groups with the help of multiplexers and demultiplexers.

Let the source S and destination 0 be represented in binary code as

$$S = sn\text{-}1\ldots\ldots\ldots\ldots s1.s0$$

$$D = dn\text{-}1\ldots\ldots\ldots\ldots d1.d0$$

The source and destinations are connected to the multiplexers and demultiplexers are as follows:

I.   If Sn-1 .. . . S1.S0 bits are the same for the two sources, then these two sources are linked through the same pair of multiplexers.

II. If dn-1 . . .. d1.do bits are the same for the two destinations, then these two destinations are linked through same pair of demultiplexer.

The ZT Network is regular in stage 2m-5 and stage 2m-l but irregular in intermediate stages. The overall design of ZT Network is irregular with 5 stages. SEs pertaining to the two groups with the same number with all the stages, except in the final stages, are connected to each other through links known as express links which are used only if the SE in next stage is busy or faulty these interconnected switches are called associative (asc) switches.

The ZT Network of size 2^n x 2^n, (where 2^n are Source, 2^n are Destination, n = $\log_2 N$, and m = $\log_2 (N/2)$) consist of $(2m - 1)$ stages and with $(2m+2 - 4)$ total no. of SEs out of which

2n-1 + 4 are of size 2x2 and rest i.e. (2n-1 + 8) are of size 3x3 connected to source and destination by 2n Multiplexer and 2n Demultiplexer. Total no. of SEs in stage 2m-5 and stage 2m-l are equal to 2n. Total no. of asc switches is 3*2n-2. Total no. of output links from stage 2m-5, stage 2m-4 and stage 2m-3 are (3 * 3N/2), total no. of output links from stage 2m-2 is N/2. Total no. of input links to stage 2m-5 and total no. of output links from stage 2m-l is (2N/2).Total no. of input links to MUX and output links from DEMUX is (2N).

Fig 7.1, Fig 7.2, and Fig. 7.3 show the construction of ZT Network for size N=16, it redundancy graph and Multipath ZT Network for size N=16 respectively.

Redundancy graph is a method of showing all possible paths between source and destination nodes on the graph represents switching elements. If the switching element belonging to the first or last stage becomes faulty then the source or the destination connected to that particular switching element will get disconnected from the network.

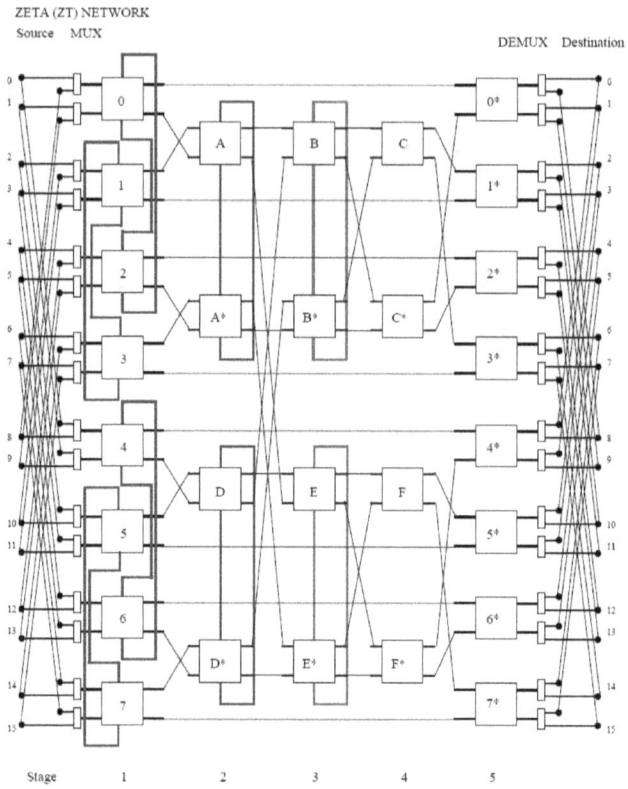

Fig. 7.1 ZETA (ZT) Network of Size 2^4 x 2^4

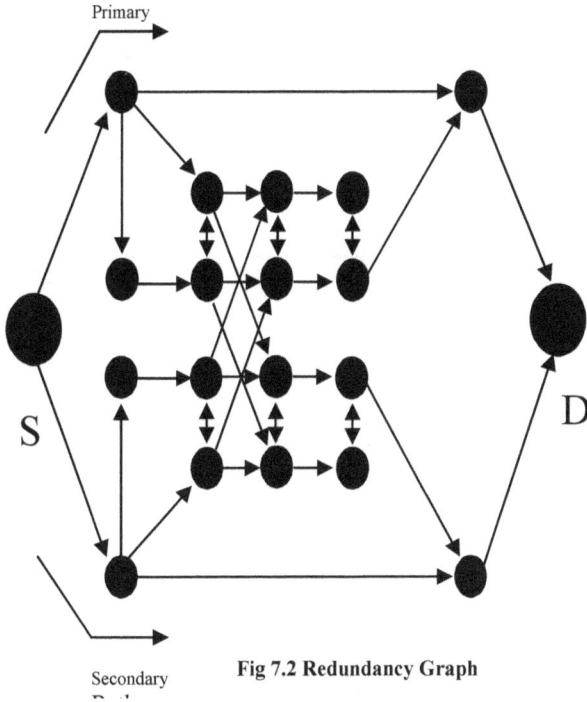

Primary

S

D

Secondary

Fig 7.2 Redundancy Graph

7.3 Routing scheme for ZETA (ZT) Network

The routing scheme for the ZT is described in this section

7.3.1 Path Length Algorithm

Algorithm: Fault Tolerant Routing for ZT Network

PROCEDURE:

S	D	Path Length available
	0000	
	0001	2,5
	1000	
	1001	
	0010	
	0011	
	0100	
0000	0101	
	0110	
	0111	5
	1010	
	1011	
	1100	
	1101	
	1110	
	1111	

I. One of subnetworks G^N based on the MSB of destination address is being selected by source for routing of data to respective destination.

II. if it is assumed that address of the following SE is known else if Destination address is address of the following SE concerning the first stage else if primary path is not faulty then it will be used by the SE to route the data from source to destination and MSB of the routing tag is 0.

III. else secondary path (i.e. intermediate path, bit dn-1 to dn of destination address) from source to   destination is used and the MSB of routing tag is 1.

IV. if SE in the intermediate stage is faulty, request passes to complementary SE in the same stage, through express link. Routing tag remains the same.

V. For routing a request through a DEMUX, use bit d0 of the routing tag.

Example 7.1

Let data be routed from source S= 0000 to various destinations D of. ZT Network.
Routing tags used and the path lengths are listed in TABLE 7.1 for N= 16.

TABLE 7.1 Routing Information for ZT Network for S=0000

7.4 Fault-Tolerance and Repair of ZETA (ZT) Network

A well known criterion used to measure the reliability of fault tolerant multistage networks is full access, i.e. the capability of the network that provides a connection from any of its input source to any of its output destination. Under the criterion of full access, a network is assumed to be faulty if there is any source-destination pair that cannot be connected because of faulty components in the network can be measured in terms of Mean Time to Failure (MTTF) of the network and / or the number of faults the network can tolerate [4,9, 11,25].

Fault Tolerance in an interconnection network is very important for continuous operation over a relatively long period of time. Fault Tolerance is the ability of the system to continue operating in the presence of faults. There are two types of fault mode is adopted to the reliability analysis of networks "switch fault" model a switch is considered to be totally unusable if it becomes faulty. While any network fault that corrupts data on information path will be called link fault. A link fault occurs in an information link when it becomes stuck at either logical "0", or "1" regardless to the actual input signal that it applied to it .The actual location of the fault can be in the link itself, an interchange box, or in the hardware interfaces of the interchange boxes that the link connects. Link faults in distributed control system can create a large numbers of network errors not found in centralized control system. These errors are due to the corruption of routing tags as they are transmitted over faulty links and the ensuing missrouting and blocking of the messages to

97

repair the Link just replace the links [12]. In this thesis a switch fault model is used for the analysis. I assumed that any of the switching components – crossbar switches, multiplexers or demultiplexers in ZT can fail. It has been assumed that faults are independent of each other.

A network is said to be a k fault tolerant if it can still provide a connection for any source-destination pair in the presence of any instance of up to k faults in the network [28].

Dynamic Fault-Tolerance in ZT has been provided by the presence of two disjoint paths at the input and output stage. In the intermediate stages, express paths in each group of a stage furnish complementary SEs, making available fault free paths leading to the destination.

A network is robust in the presence of k faults if it can tolerate some instances of k faults. The maximum number of faults it can tolerate comes from the case that only one of the groups is fault free [28]. So ZT Network is robust up to [N + (2m-l - 2)].

Theorem 7.1: *ZT is single switch fault tolerant in stage 2m-5, stage 2m-4 and stage 2m-3.*

Proof: two paths are available through each stage for any given source-destination pair involving either of asc SEs. Considering that the destinations to be fault free, at least one path is usable to pass data through that particular source-destination involving a single switch failure.

Theorem 7.2: *Even if the conjugate SEs, in a loop within the first group, in first stage is simultaneously faulty Even then the data can be routed to destination in ZT*

98

Proof: The secondary path is used in the event of failure of primary path. The multiplexer attached with the secondary group SEs will help the data to reach its specified destination through intermediate stages. All SEs work intelligently i.e. in the event of failure of its successive SE the later SE will route the data to its specified destination with the help of auxiliary path, this is known as adaptive routing.

Theorem 7.3: *ZT will be able to work in the event when one of the group is completely faulty.*

Proof: All permutation will pass through the second group in the event that first group is completely faulty.

Lemma 7.1: *In ZT if all the associative switches in both groups in stage 2m-5, 2m-4, and 2m-3 are simultaneously faulty, then clearly ZT fails.*

To rectify this fault just Replace the loop involving the faulty component with new one.

7.5 Performance Analysis of ZETA (ZT) Network

In this section, the performance of ZT is analyzed under fault free condition.

7.5.1 Parameters

The following five-performance metrics are used to evaluate

the performance of the ZT Network.

I.   Bandwidth
for $a^n \times b^n$ is given by

$$BW = b^n p^n$$

II.   Probability of
acceptance for $a^n \times b^n$ is
given by

$$Pa = bn\ qn\ /\ an\ q \text{ or } Pa = BW/an\ p$$

99

III.   Throughput (TP) for $a^n \times b^n$ is given by

$$TP = BW / a^n T \text{ or } PU \times p$$

IV.   Processor Utilization (PU) for $a^n \times b^n$ is given by

$$PU = BW / a^n p T$$

V.   Processing Power (PP) for $a^n \times b^n$ is giveg, by

$$PP = a^n \times PU$$

7.5.2 ZETA (ZT) Network

It is seen that in case of ZT, the input and output stages have N/2 SEs each whereas each of the intermediate stages have the same number of N/4 SEs. Probability of request reaching the final stage will depend on the route taken by the packet to reach the destination. When the request reaches the final stage directly, path length is 2. But in event that it passes through the intermediate stages; maximum path length of $[(\log_2 N) + 1]$ is adapted. Thus $a=b=2$ and $n=4$ for a 16×16 ZT Network. Bandwidth is computed from the following expression:

$$BW = b^n \, P_n = (2^n \, P_{n+2}$$
$$(2^n \, P_{n-3}) / 8$$

$P_n s$ are calculated as under

$$P_{n+2} = 1 - \{ (1 - P_{n+1}/2) (1 - P_{n-3}/2) \}$$

$$P_{n+1} = 1 - \{ (1 - P_n/2) (1 - P_{n-1}/2) (1 - P_{n-2}/2) (1 - P_{n-3}/2) \}$$

$$P_n = 1 - \{ (1 - P_{n-1}/2)^2 (1 - P_{n-2}/2) (1 - P_{n-3}/2) \}$$

and

$$Po = P$$

where p is the memory request rate and it varies over different paths having different path length.

The Probability of acceptance:

$$Pa = BW/a^n \, P = P_{n-}$$

$$_2/4p + P_{n-3}/8p$$

The Processor Utilization:

$$PU =$$

$$BW/an\ pT =$$

$$Pn\text{-}zl4pT +$$

$$Pn\_3/8pT$$

As T is variable in ZT, PU varies
depending on the path chosen

The Processing Power:

$$PP = 2n \times PU = 2n$$

$$Pn+Z\ 14pT + 2n$$

$$Pn\text{-}3\ 18pT$$

The Throughput:

$$PU = BW/an\ pT = Pn\text{-}zl4pT + Pn\_3/8pT$$

A computer program in C++ language has been developed and the values calculated are tabulated below

$P_{request\ generation.}$	BW	Pa	PU	PP	TP
0.1	1.0203	0.637686	0.212562	3.40099	0.021256 2
0.2	1.72534	0.539169	0.179723	2.87557	0.035944 6
0.3	2.24942	0.46863	0.15621	2.49936	0.046863
0.4	2.66311	0.41611	0.138703	2.21926	0.055481 4
0.5	3.00483	0.375604	0.125201	2.00322	0.062600 7
0.6	3.29633	0.343368	0.114456	1.8313	0.068673 6
0.7	3.55032	0.316993	0.105664	1.69063	0.073965
0.8	3.7745	0.294883	0.0982942	1.57271	0.078635 3
0.9	3.97366	0.275949	0.0919829	1.47173	0.082784 6
1.0	4.1509	0.259431	0.086477	1.38363	0.086477

TABLE 7.2 Performance Parameters for
ZT Network with N=16

P request generation.	BW	Pa	PU	PP	TP
0.1	0.9798	0.6123	0.1749	2.7948	0.0175
0.2	1.6792	0.5247	0.1499	2.3984	0.0299
0.3	2.2118	0.4607	0.1316	2.0156	0.0394
0.4	2.6332	0.4114	0.1175	1.8800	0.0470
0.5	2.9826	0.3728	0.1065	1.7040	0.0532
0.6	3.2792	,0.3415	0.0975	1.5600	0.0585
0.7	3.5374	0.3158	0.0902	1.4432	0.0631
0.8	3.7644	0.2940	0.0840	1.3440	0.0672
0.9	3.9654	0.2753	0.0786	1.2576	0.0707
1.0	4.1440	0.2590	0.0740	1.1840	0.0740

TABLE 7.3 Performance Parameters for ALN Network with N=16

P request generation.	BW	Pa	PU	PP	TP
0.1	0.868779	0.542987	0.180996	2.89593	0.0180996
0.2	1.5354	0.479811	0.159937	2.55899	0.0319874
0.3	2.0648	0.430167	0.143389	2.29422	0.0430167
0.4	2.49836	0.390369	0.130123	2.08197	0.0520492
0.5	2.86267	0.357835	0.119278	1.90845	0.059639
0.6	3.17504	0.330735	0.110245	1.76391	0.0661467
0.7	3.44687	0.307756	0.1 02585	1.64137	0.718098
0.8	3.68576	0.28795	0.0959833	1.53573	0.0767866
0.9	3.89686	0.270615	0.090205	1.44328	0.0811845
1.0	4.0837	0.255231	0.085077	1.36123	0.085077

TABLE 7.4 Performance Parameters for PHI Network with N=16

P request-generation.	BW	Pa	PU	PP	TP
0.1	0.923981	0.577488	0.192496	3.07994	0.0192496
0.2	1.71819	0.536934	0.178978	2.86365	0.0357956
0.3	2.40921	0.501919	0.167306	2.6769	0.0501919
0.4	3.01656	0.471338	0.157113	2.5138	0.0628451
0.5	3.55465	0.444332	0.148111	2.36977	0.0740553
0.6	4.03415	0.420224	0.140075	2.24119	0.0840778
0.7	4.46301	0.398483	0.132828	2.12524	0.0929793
0.8	4.84716	0.378685	0.126228	2.01965	0.100983
0.9	5.1911	0.360493	0.120164	1.92263	0.108148
1.0	5.49818	0.343636	0.114545	1.83275	0.114545

TABLE 7.5 Performance Parameters for THN Network with N=16

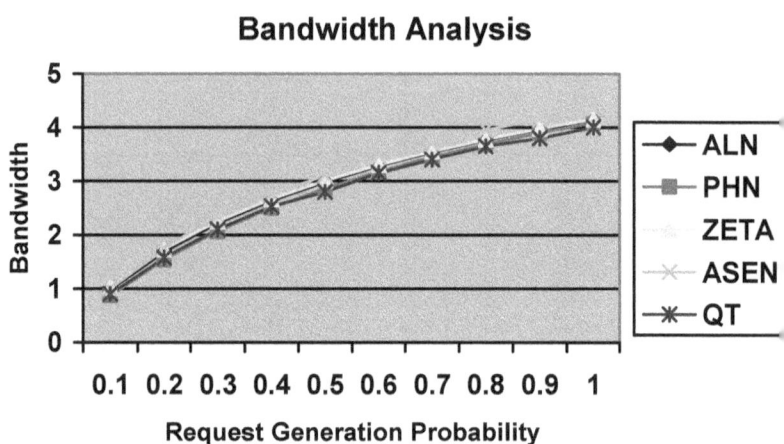

Fig 7.4(a) Comparative Bandwidth

Pa Analysis

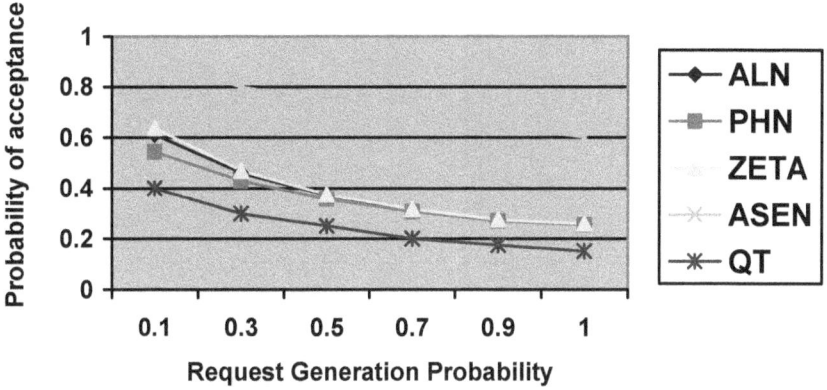

Fig 7.4(b) Comparative Probability of Acceptance

PU Analysis

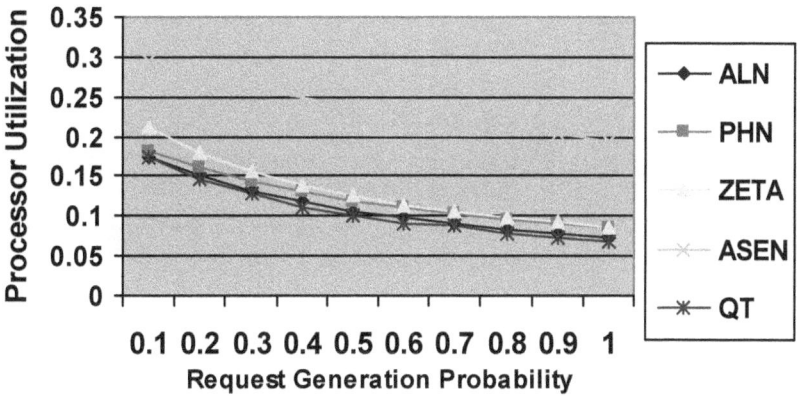

Fig 7.4(c) Comparative Processor utilization

PP Analysis

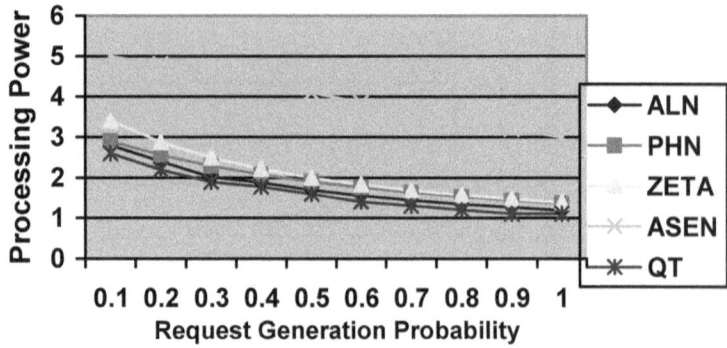

Fig 7.4(d) Comparative Processing Power

TP Analysis

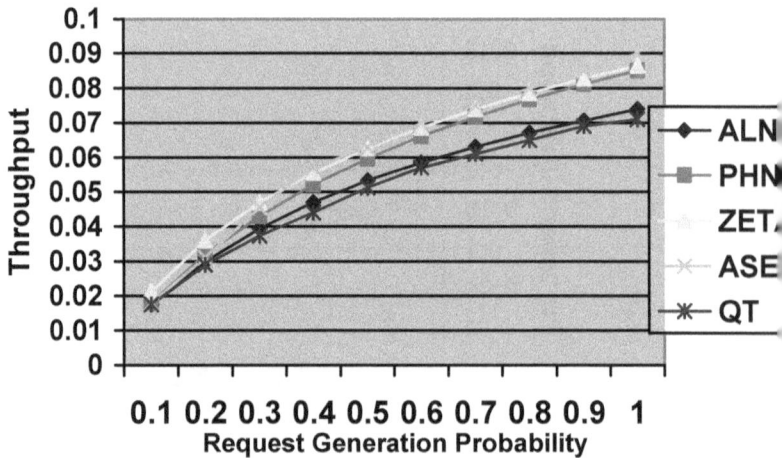

Fig 7.4(e) Comparative Throughput

The tables [TABLE 7.2-7.5] show the values of different performance measures metrics for different values of P $_{request-generation}$ (i.e. Probability of Request-Generation) from the tables [TABLE 7.2- 7.5] it has been depicted and analyzed that for all the networks, as the P $_{request\ generation}$ increases the Bandwidth (BW) and Throughput (TP) increases because more number of packets are delivered to the destination from source but the values for Probability of acceptance (Pa), Processing Power (PP) and Processor Utilization (PU) decreases as P $_{request-generation}$ increases that is due to contention among the switches increases. The average time taken to route a packet, between a source-destination pair for best case for PHI is 3 .0, for THN is 3.0, for ALN is 3.5 and for ZT it is same as 3.5. The network size for all the above mentioned cases are a=b=2, n=4. The increase and decrease in various performance measures can be shown by different graphs presented in Fig. 7.4(a), Fig. 7.4(b), Fig. 7.4(c), Fig. 7.4(d), and Fig. 7.4(e).

The gain in overall performance as regards to ZT over PHI ,and ALN is obvious from Fig. 7.4(a), Fig. 7.4(b), Fig. 7.4(c), Fig. 7.4(d), and Fig. 7.4(e). The Bandwidth of ZT is higher than PHI and ALN as available paths for the delivery of packets to the destination are much more than in the later, as can be seen in Fig. 7.4(a). Fig. 7.4(b) exhibits higher Probability of acceptance for ZT, which is above PHI and ALN. Processor Utilization, shown in Fig. 7.4(c) shows an improvement as more SEs are being made active for the transfer of data. Processing Power, Fig. 7.4(d) is enhanced as in totality more SEs are activated, providing additional paths. Since increased number of packets is accepted at the destination per unit cycle in ZT, throughput also shows considerable improvement, as depicted in Fig. 7.4(e). Even though ZT is of 5 stages it has high performance values than PHI, has 4 stages.

7.6 RELIABILITY of ZETA (ZT) Network - Mean Time to Failure

As the acceptance and use of multiprocessor system grows, reliability of the interconnection network needs increased attention. Analysis of reliability to ZT follows similar procedure as has been provided in chapter 7.

The following are the basic steps and the estimated individual reliability factors are identified factors [9].

I.   First, elements, subsystem and the estimated individual reliability factors are identified.

II.   Next a block diagram representing the logical manner in which these elements are

connected is prepared to form the system.

III.   Then condition for the successful operation of the system is determined i.e. it is

decided that how many units should function.

IV.   Finally the combinational rules of probability theory i.e. add, multiply and their

combinations are applied to arrive at the system reliability factor.

The following assumption are made during the analysis

All the switching elements are not dependent on each other. So it means failure of any switch doesn't affect the reliability of other.

The failure of switch occurs independently in a network with a failure rate of $(A = 10'6$ per hour) permit time. Based on the Gate count, failure rate for a 2x2 SE, $\lambda_2 = \lambda$ and for a 3x3 SE, $\lambda_3 = 2.25 \lambda$ for mxl MUX $\lambda_m (=\lambda_d) = \lambda/4 * m =$ failure rate of lxm DEMUX where λ_m failure rate of MUX, λ_d failure rate of DEMUX, λ_2 failure rate of 2x2 SE, λ_3 failure rate of 3x3 SE [6, 7, 9, **11,25**].

7.6.1 Upper Bound of MTTF

The MTTF of ZT can be analyzed by defining a critical set of components. A critical set of components is defined as the set of m+ I switching components each from different groups, such that a network failure will occur if all the m+ 1 components become faulty simultaneously. It is observed that each source is connected to multiplexers in both the subnetworks [28]. Thus ZT is operational as long as one of the two to a source in either subnetwork is operational. Reliability block dia 7.5 (a). The value for Upper Bound of MTTF for ZT Network is p and MTTF for Other Networks are given in

(Table 7.7, 7.8, and 4 Time- To-Failure for Upper bound of ZT is computed as follows:

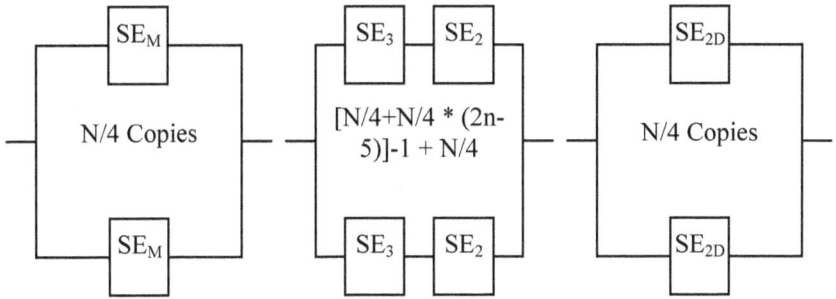

Fig. 7.5(a) Block diagram
for Upper Bound of
reliability

$$R_{ZT\_UB}(t) =$$
$$[\,1-(\,1-e^{-\lambda_m t}\,)^2\,]^{N/4}.\,[\,1-(\,1-e^{-\lambda_3 t}\,e^{-\lambda_2 t}\,)(\,1-e^{-\lambda_3 t}\,e^{-\lambda_2 t}\,)\,]^{[N/}$$
$$.\,[\,1-(\,1-e^{-\lambda_{2d} t}\,)^2\,]^{N/4}$$

Size	16	32	64	128	256	512	102
VB	137000	87109	57488	38831	26675	18580	131

TABLE 7.6 Upper Bound of MTTF for ZT Network

Size	16	32	64	128	256	512	102
VB	136078	86187	56566	37909	25753	17658	121

TABLE 7.7 Upper Bound of MTTF for ALN Network

Size	16	32	64	128	256	512	1024
VB	134935	77685	47339	29855	19255	1261	8353

TABLE 7.8 Upper Bound of MTTF for ASEN 2 Network

Size	16	32	64	128	256	512	102
UB	143302	92715	61667	41680	28567	20744	137

TABLE 7.9 Upper Bound of MTTF for QT Network

or Lower Bound each group is considered independently and is assumed to be faulty if there is any single fault in it. Since at the input side of ZT, routing scheme does not consider the multiplexers to be the integral part of the 2x2 switch. Hence, if both multiplexers are grouped with each switch in the input side and regarded as a series system, then the conservative estimate of reliability [28], shown in block diagram of Fig. 7.5 (b), is obtained. The value for Lower Bound of MTTF for ZT Network is provided in Table 7.10 and

MTTF for Other Networks are given in (Table 7.11, and 7.12 [25]). The

Mean- Time- To-Failure for lower bound of ZT is computed as:

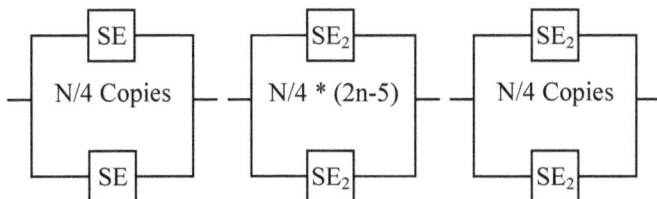

Fig. 7.5(b) Block diagram for Lower Bound of reliability

$$R_{ZT\bar{L}B}(t) =$$
$$[1-(1-e^{-\lambda_m t})^2]^{N/4} \cdot [1-(1-e^{-\lambda_2 t})^2]^{N/4 \cdot (2n-5)} \cdot [1-(1-e^{-\lambda_{2d} t})^2]^{N/4}$$

$$MTTF_{ZT\_LB} = \int_0^{\infty} \sim_{\_LB}(t). \, dt$$

Size	16	32	64	128	256	512	1024
LB	117616	74392	48691	32540	22049	15083	1039

TABLE 7.10 Lower Bound of MTTF for ZT Network

Size	16	32	64	128	256	512	1024
LB	118383	69950	43375	27700	18035	1190	7928

TABLE 7.11 Lower Bound of MTTF for ASEN-2 Network

Size	16	32	64	128	256	512	1024
LB	123710	80347	53604	36341	24955	17277	12113

TABLE 7.12 Lower Bound of MTTF for QT Network

Upper bound MTTF for minimum path length

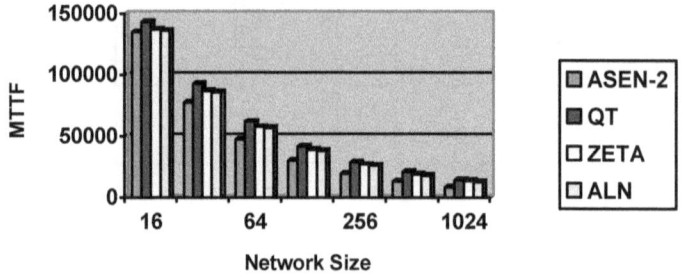

Fig 7.6(a) Comparative Upper Bound MTTF of related MINs

Lower bound MTTF for minimum path length

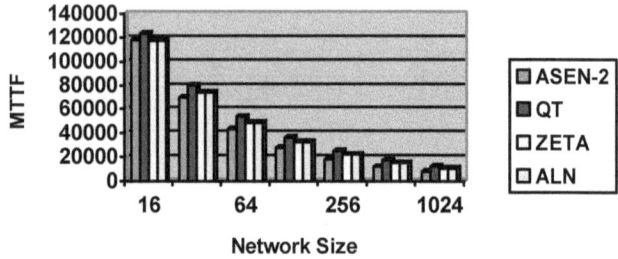

Fig 7.6(b) Comparative Lower Bound MTTF of related MINs

Relative variations in Upper Bound of MTTF of ZT, ALN, QT, and ASEN-2 Networks are shown in Fig. 7.6(a). The difference in reliability of the four MINs indicates that for a small network size, Upper Bound MTTF of ZT, ALN, and ASEN-2 Networks is about the same, but as the size increases ZT Network has an edge over ASEN-2 and ALN Networks which implies that ZT is more reliable in comparison to ALN and ASEN-2 Network.

Now Relative variations in Lower Bound of MTTF of ZT, ALN, QT, and ASEN-2 Networks are shown in Fig. 7.6(b). The difference in reliability of the four MINs indicates that for a small as well as large network sizes, Lower Bound MTTF of ZT is higher than that of ASEN-2 Network, which again implies that ZT is more reliable in comparison to ASEN-2 Network. Lower Bound MTTF of ZT is less than that of QT Network, which again implies that ZT is less reliable in comparison to QT Network and Lower Bound of MTTF of ZT and ALN Networks are same.

7.7 Cost-Effectiveness

It is observed that ZT network can provide competitive reliability as compared to other fault-tolerant MINs considered for the study. However, if such high reliability comes at the expense of high cost, it may have little value in practice. In this section, the cost of different networks is computed and compared for different network size.

Considering that a 2x2 switch has four units of hardware cost, a 3x3 switch has nine units of cost mx 1 multiplexer and 1 xm demultiplexer have m units of cost-depending on the gate count, the cost function of different networks with their cost for respective sizes are given in the Table 7.13. The hardware cost of ZT Network is comes out to be $N/8[56+2410giN/2)]$, Where is N is a Network Size.

Networks	Cost Function	N=16	N=32	N=64	N=128	N=256	N=512	N=1024
ALN	$N/2[17+910gi^{N/2})]$	352	848	1984	4544	10240	22784	50176
ZT	$N/8[56+2410giN/2)$	256	608	1408	3200	7168	15872	34816
ESC	$2N(log_2^{N+5})$	288	640	1408	3072	6656	14336	30720
3-replicate	$6N(log_2^{N})$	384	960	2304	5376	12288	27648	61440
INDRA	$4N(log_2N+1)$	320	768	1792	4096	9216	20480	45056
ASEN-2	$3N(1.5\ log_2N-1)$	240	624	1536	3648	8448	19200	43008
ABN	$(9n-ll)N/2$	200	544	1376	3328	7808	17920	40448
QT	$9.75 * 2n+l-54$	258	570	1194	2442	4938	9930	19914

Cost Value for different sizes

TABLE No. 7.13 Comparative Cost analysis of different Networks

From Table 7.13 and from Fig. 7.7, it can be depicted and analyzed that when irregular networks are compared the cost of 16x 16 ZT Network is less then the cost of QT Network for same size, but as the size increases the cost of ZT is more than the cost of QT but less than the cost of ALN. Now from Fig. 7.7(b) it is noticed that for designing higher size networks i.e. (N=128, 256, 512, 1024) the ZT comes out to be more

economical as compared to others as the cost of ZT, is less, when compared

with ABN, ASEN-2, AND ALN for the sizes (N=128, 256,512, 1024). And

from Fig. 7.7(c) and 7.7(d) the cost ofZT is also comes out to be less, than the

cost of ABN, ASEN-2, INDRA with R=2, ALN, and 3-replicated Networks

for all the sizes of networks i.e. (N=16, 32, 64,128,256,512,1024).

Cost Analysis

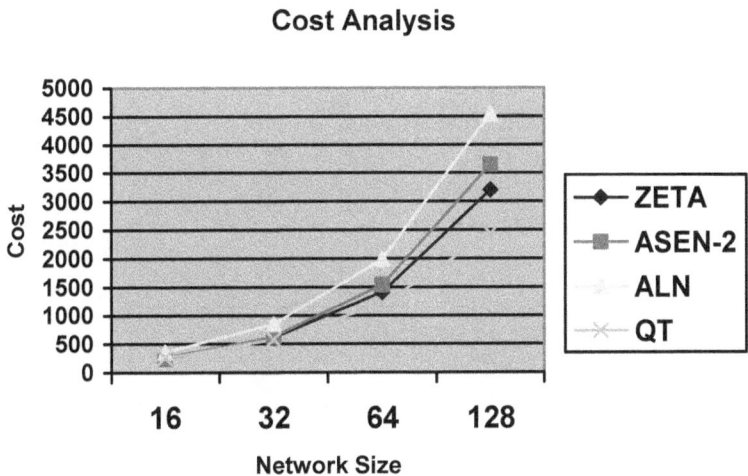

Fig 7.7(a) Comparative Cost of related MINs

Cost Analysis

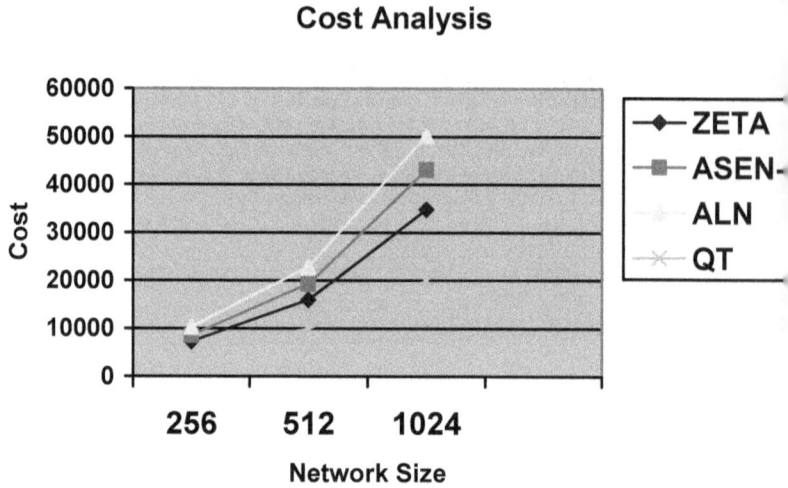

Fig 7.7(b) Comparative Cost of related MINs

7.8 Comparison with related MINs

7.8.1 Performance

Performance comparison of these three MINs makes evident the overall superiority of ZT over ALN and PHI. As from tables [Table 7.2 - 7.5] and from figures [Fig. 7.4(a) - (e)] it is clear that the Bandwidth, Probability of acceptance, Processor Utilization, Processing Power, and Throughput for ZT Network is higher than that of ALN, and PHI network.

Reason being the routing capability of irregular ZT confirms that 50% of the requests are passed by using the minimum path length of 2, reducing the latency drastically as compared to the irregular ALN and PHI Networks. Remaining requests utilize the normal regular route, where path length is $[(1og_2N) + 1]$. PHI also provides the minimum path length of 2, but ZT being regular in the intermediate stages, makes available more redundant paths, improving its performance on the whole.

7.8.2 Reliability

From Fig. 7.6(a) it is depicted that the Upper Bound of MTTF of ZT Network is more than that of ALN and ASEN-2 Network, but less than that of QT Network and from Fig. 7.6(b) it is clear that the Lower Bound of MTTF for ZT Network comes out to be more than that of ASEN-2 Network, but less than that of QT Network. Lower Bound of MTTF of ZT and ALN Networks are same.

The reason being that as the size increases, the number of SEs in ASEN-2 becomes very high, increasing the probability of finding a failed component on the path to the destination. This probability is very less in QT as it is irregular and no. of SEs in the intermediate stages is considerably less. ZT keeps a moderate approach being irregular at the input-output stages, and regular in the intermediate stages.

7.8.3 Cost

From Table 7.13 and from Fig. 7.7, it can be depicted and analyzed that when irregular networks are compared the cost of 16x 16 ZT Network is less than the cost of QT Network for same size, but as the size increases the cost of ZT is more than the cost of QT but less than the cost of ALN for all network sizes. Reason being that the ZT has more no. of SEs in intermediate stage as compared with QT but ZT has no chaining links in second last stage which makes it less costlier than the ALN Network. Now from Fig. 7.7(b) it is noticed that for designing higher size network i.e. for (N=128, 256, 512, 1024) the ZT come out to be more economical as compared to others as the cost of ZT, is less, when compared with ABN, ASEN-2, AND ALN for the sizes (N=128, 256, 512, 1024). Reason being that ZT is irregular in nature and has less no. of SEs in intermediate stage. And from Fig. 7.7(c) and 7.7(d) the cost of ZT is comes out to be less, than the cost of ABN, ASEN-2, INDRA with R=2, ALN, and 3-replicated Networks for the all sizes i.e. for (N=16, 32, 64, 128,256,512, 1024).

7.9 CONCLUSION

A Fault Tolerant, Irregular, Dynamic, and Cost-Effective Hybrid Network has been proposed for Irregular Multistage Interconnection Networks, named as ZETA (ZT) Network. This network integrates all the benefits of regular and irregular character of MINs, exhibiting better latency and performance over Fault- Tolerant, irregular, dynamic ALN and PHI networks explained in section 7.5. The ZT Network is more reliable or has more value of MTTF for

Upper Bound and Lower Bound in event of failures over FaultTolerant, irregular, dynamic ALN and Fault- Tolerant, regular, and dynamic, ASEN-2 explained in section 7.6. The ZT Network is very cost effective in comparison with other similar MINs. The Cost- Effectiveness of ZT compared to existing ALN, ASEN, ABN, INORA with R=2, and 3-replicated Networks makes it a better candidate to be used in the parallel processing environment when economy is concerned.

Thus ZT network maintains the benefit of both regular and irregular characteristics of MINs and presents superior reliability (calculated in terms of Upper Bound and Lower Bound), low cost (calculated in terms of hardware), and low latency while maintaining good performance (calculated in terms of Bandwidth, Probability of acceptance, processor Utilization, Processing Power, and Throughput).

CHAPTER 8 CONCLUSIONS AND FUTURE SCOPE OF WORK

8.1 CONCLUSION

This thesis addresses the need and importance of multistage interconnection networks. Designing a multistage interconnection network is very critical because it has a great impact on the system capabilities i.e. its performance, reliability, permutation passabiliy and cost. The optimization of these factors is required for the sustained operation of the network and hence it involves trade-off between these factors. Fault-tolerance capability in these MINs helps them to operate even under certain faults. Hence, various different techniques have been employed to increase the performance of these MINs. Some are based on providing redundancy and some use chaining among the switches so as to provide alternative paths.

A new class of irregular, fault-tolerant multistage interconnection network named Irregular Augmented Shuffle Network (IASN) has been proposed in this thesis. The network uses 2 x 2 SEs and 3 x 3 SEs which results in reduction of stages. The network being irregular supports multiple paths of varied path lengths with minimum path length of 2 in comparison to the regular networks that have a fixed path length. Average latency in the network is considerably lowered as 50% of the requests pass through minimum path length of 2. The remaining requests pass through the path length of ($\log_2 N$-l). Regular Networks have a fixed path length, which increases the latency as the network size increases as same delay is encountered by all the requests. The routing algorithm provides efficient routing capabilities even under presence of faults. The network has been provided fault-tolerant capability by using auxiliary links between the switches in the each stage except the last one. This helps to route requests even in presence of faults by using the alternative routes available.

Various performance parameters have been analyzed and compared with various existing networks. The performance analysis of IASN shows better performance of the network in comparison to various existing networks. The reliability analysis of the network depicts improved reliability of the network as compared with some of the existing networks like ASEN-2 and ABN. And it is comparably reliable with the irregular FT network. The IASN network is cost-effective too in comparison to other existing ASEN-2, ABN, INDRA, ESC networks. This feature also indicates superiority of IASN network because better performance, reliability at the expense of high cost is not preferred.

The permutation passability, depicting the identity as well as incremental permutations of IASN, shows that IASN has better permutation passability in comparison to network like ASEN-2, ABN and FT network. 50% of the requests pass through minimum path length of 2 and moreover, remaining requests pass through the normal route of path length equal to $(\log_2 N\text{-}1)$. Hence, the average path length of IASN is less in comparison to FT network. This helps in reducing the latency.

Routing messages in a multistage network in the presence of faults allows the system to be kept operational until a repair can be scheduled. Thus the approach is highly suited to systems where the probability of fault during the period of interest is very small to justify the expense of providing redundant hardware, but tolerance to single faults is essential.

ZETA network integrates all the benefits of regular and irregular character of MINs, exhibiting better latency and performance over Fault- Tolerant, irregular, dynamic ALN and PHI networks.

To sum up briefly, the proposed irregular, fault-tolerant MIN offers various desirable features to be used in high performance parallel computing systems.

8.2 FUTURE SCOPE OF WORK

- Search for new topological design and analysis of static and dynamic, regular and irregular MINs with an aim towards increased performance and reliability.

- VLSI implementation of the proposed network.

- The use of MINs in ATM applications can be explored.

- Examination of the problems arising from the use of large switching elements is needed.

- Energy Savings with appropriate interconnection networks in parallel DSP needs further exploration.

APPENDEX – I : REFERENCES

[I] Adams G.B., Aggarwal D.P. and Siegel H.I, " A Survey and Comparison of Fault-tolerant Interconnection Networks", DEEE Computers, Vol. 20, June 1987, pp. 14-27,

[2] Adams EH G.B. and Siegel H.J., " The Extra Stage Cube: A Fault Tolerant Interconnection Network for Supersystems", IEEE Transactions on Computer, 1982, pp. 443-454.

[3] Anderson G.A., Jensen E.D,, "Computer Interconnection Networks: Taxonomy, Characteristics and Examples", ACM Computing Surveys, Vol. 7, Dec. 1975, pp. 197-213

[4] Balaguruswamy. E., "Reliability Engineering", TataMc-Graw Hill, 1989.

[5] Bansal P.K., Singh K. and Joshi R.C., "Fault-Tolerant Double Tree Network", Proc. of International Conférence IEEE INFOCOM 91, April, pp. 462-468

[6] Bansal P.K., Singh K. and Joshi R.C., "Routing and Path Length for a Cost-Effective Four tree Multistage Interconnection Network", International Journal of Electronics and Electrical Engineering, Vol 73, No.l, 1992, pp. 107-115.

[7] Bansal Savina and Bansal P.K., "Performance and Reliability Analysis for a Multistage Interconnection Network", presented in NSC-93 atIIT Kanpur, Dec. 1993.

[8] Bansal P.K., Singh K. and Joshi R.C., "On a Fault-Tolerant Multistage Interconnection Network", International Journal of Electronics and Electrical Engineering, Vol 20, N0.4, 1994, pp. 335-345.

[9] Booting C, Rai S. and Agarwal D.P., "Reliability • Computation' of "Multistage Interconnection Networks", IEEE Transactions on Reliability, Vol. 38, No. 1,1994, pp. 13-8-145.

[10] Duato J., Yalmanchili S. and Ni L.M., "Interconnection Networks: An 'Engineering Approach", IEEE Computer Society, 1997.

[II] Feng T.Y., "Survey of Interconnection Networks", IEEE Computers, Vol. 4, Dec. 1981, pp. 12-27.

[12] Howard J. Siegel, Wayne G. Nation, Cylde P. Kruskal and Leonard M. Napolitano, "Using the Multistage Cube Network Topology in Parallel Supercomputers", Proceedings of IEEE, Vol. 77, No, 12, Dec. 1979, pp. 1932-1953.

[13]Hwang Kai, "Advanced Parallel Processing with Super Computers", Proc. DEEE OC-75,Oct 1987, pp. 127-137.[14] Hwang Kai, and Faye A. Briggs, "Computer Architecture and Parallel Processing", Mc-GrawHill, 1998.

[14] Hwang Kai, and Faye A. Briggs, "Computer Architecture and Parallel Processing", Mc-GrawHill, 1998.

[15]Kumar V.P. and Reddy S.M., "Augmented Shuffle Exchange Multistage Interconnection Network", IEEE Computer, June 1987, pp.30-40,

[16]Lawrie D.H., "Access and Alignment of Data in an Array Processor", IEEE Transactions on Computers, VoL C-24, Dec. 1975, pp. 1145-1155.

[17] Levitt N., Green M.W. and Goldberg J., "A Study Communication Problem in the Self-Repairable Multiprocessor", Proc. AFIPS Conference, VoL 32, 1968,

[18] Liu M.T., "Distributed Loop Computer Networks"; Advances in Computers, VoL 17, 1978, pp. 163-221.

[19]Mudge T.N., Hayes J.P. and Winsor D.C, "Multiple Bus Architecture", IEEE Computers, June 1987, pp. 42-48.

[20]Patel J.H., "Performance of Prpcessor-Memory Interconnections for Multiprocessors", IEEE Transactions on Computers, Vol. 30,1981, pp. 771-780.

[21]Raghavandera C.S. and Verma A., "INDRA: A Class of Interconnection Networks with Redundant Paths", Proc. Real-Time Systems Symposium, Dec, 1984, pp. 153-164.

[22] Sengupta Jyotsna, "On Fault-Tolerant Multistage Interconnection Networks", Ph.D, thesis, Thapar Institute of Engg. and Technology, Patiala, June 2001.

[23] Siegel H.J.and Mcmillan R.L, "Using the Augmented Data Manipulator Network in PASM", IEEE Computer, Vol. 4, No. 2, Feb. 1981.

[24] Siegel H.J., "Interconnection Network for Large Scale Parallel Processing: Theory and Case Studies", Mc-Graw Hill, 1990.

[25] Stone H.S., "Parallel Processing with Perfect Shuffle", EEE Transactions on Computers, VoL C-20,Feb. 1971, pp. 153-161.

[26]Wei S. and Lee. G, "Extra Group Network: A Cost Effective Fault-Tolerant Multistage Interconnection Network", Proceedings of 15th Annual Symposium on Computer Architecture, May 1988, pp. 108-115.

[27]Tzeng N, Yew P. and Zhu C., "A Fault-Tolerant Scheme for Multistage Interconnection Networks'V 12th International Symposium on Computer Architecture, 1985, pp. 368-375.

28]Varma A. and Raghavandera C.S., "Fault-Tolerant Routing in Multistage Interconnection Networks", IEEE Transactions on Computers, Vol. 38, No. 3, March 1989, pp. 385-393.

[29] Wittie L.D., "Communication Structures for Large Networks of Microcomputers",
IEEE Transactions on Computers, Vol. 30, April 1981, pp. 264-273
[30] Wu C. and Feng T., "On a class of Multistage Interconnection Networks" , IEEE Transactions on Computers, 1980 , pp. 696 - 702

APPENDEX – II : PUBLICATIONS

1). Sadawarti H.K., Bansal P.K. , "An Efficient Interconnection Augmented Shuffle Network", WSEAS Transaction on Communication, ISSUE 3, VOL-6, MARCH 2007,

ISSN 1109-2742, pp 486-491

www.worldses.org/journals/communications/communications-march2007.doc

2) Sadawarti H.K., Bansal P.K "Fault diagnosis in Multiple-path interconnection Network", GESJ Georgian Electronic Scientific Journal : Computer Science and Telecommunication 2006./ No. 219,pp 146-153

3) Sadawarti H.K., Bansal P.K "Fault-tolerant Routing in Unique-path Multistage Interconnection Networks" OPEN J-GATE Journal : Computer Sciences and Telecommunications No. 4254 Open Access Journal.

4) "Unique Path Multistage Interconnection Network", IEEE INDICON 2003, IIT Kharagpur, Dec 20-22, 2004, pp 427-430.

5) "Fault Tolerant Irregular Augmented Shuffle Network" International Conference on High Performance Computing HIPC, Bangalore, Dec 2004.

6) "Survey of Interconnection Networks in Parallel Processing", International conference on Challenges in Networking & future of e-commerce, APIIT, Panipat, 9-10 April 2005, pp 237-255.

7) "Routing in Interconnection Networks" International Conference on Information Technology CIT 2004, Dec 2004 Hyderabad, pp 168-174.

APPENDEX – III: ABOUT AUTHOR

Harsh Sadawarti received the B.E. Degree in Computer Technology from **Nagpur University**, Nagpur, India in 1994 & M.E. in Computer Science & Engineering from **Thapar Institute of Engineering & Technology, Patiala, India.** India in 2000. In 1994 he joined the Computer Industry for 2 years as Customer Support Engineer. In July 1996 he joined as **Lecturer in Computer Science & Engineering at BBSB Engineering College, Fatehgarh Sahib,India.** In 2001 he joined as **Asstt Professor cum Head of Deptt at RIMT-Institute of Management & Computer Technology, Mandi Gobindgarh, India.** He is currently **Vice-Principal & Professor in Deptt of Computer Science & Engineering at RIMT-Institute of Engineering & Technology, Mandi Gobindgarh, India.** He is Pursuing his Ph.D in Computer Science & Engineering. His research interests are Computer Architecture, Parallel Processing, Computer Networks, Parallel & Distributed Systems.

APPENDEX – IV: INDEX

www.ingramcontent.com/pod-product-compliance
Lightning Source LLC
Chambersburg PA
CBHW031944190326
41519CB00007B/652